READING
science

READING
science

Practical Strategies for Integrating Instruction

Jennifer L. Altieri

HEINEMANN
Portsmouth, NH

Heinemann
361 Hanover Street
Portsmouth, NH 03801–3912
www.heinemann.com

Offices and agents throughout the world

© 2016 by Jennifer L. Altieri

The author and publisher wish to thank those who have generously given permission to reprint borrowed material:

Figure 3.2: Useful Morphemes from "Getting to the Root of Word Study" by Nancy Padak, Evangeline Newton, Timothy Rasinski, and Rick M. Newton in *What Research Has to Say About Vocabulary Instruction* by Alan E. Farstrup and S. Jay Samuels, Editors. Copyright © 2008 by the International Reading Association, Inc. Reprinted with permission from the International Reading Association conveyed via the Copyright Clearance Center.

Figure 4.1: Informational Text Features from *Powerful Content Connections: Nurturing Readers, Writers, and Thinkers in Grades K–3* by Jennifer Altieri. Copyright © 2014 by the International Reading Association, Inc. Reprinted with permission from the International Reading Association conveyed via the Copyright Clearance Center.

Figure 5.1 Parts of an Atom, Figure 5.2 Life Cycle of an Apple Tree, and Figure 5.3 Decibel Levels of Various Sounds from *Science Magnifier* (2010). Published by Carolina Biological Supply Company. Reprinted with permission from the publisher, www.carolina.com.

Image credits: Figure 5.2 (left to right): © Houghton Mifflin Harcout/HIP; © CW Images/Alamy/HIP; © Liquidlibrary/Jupiterimages/Getty Images/HIP. Figure 5.3 (left to right): © Barbara Penoyer/Photodisc/Getty Images/HIP; © Corbis/HIP

Cataloging-in-Publication data is on file at the Library of Congress.
ISBN: 978-0-325-06258-7

Editor: Katherine Bryant
Production: Victoria Merecki
Cover design: Suzanne Heiser
Interior design: Shawn Girsberger
Typesetter: Shawn Girsberger
Manufacturing: Steve Bernier

Printed in the United States of America on acid-free paper
20 19 18 17 16 PPC 1 2 3 4 5

To Ashu

*and the teachers
who will encourage
his scientific interest and passion*

Contents

Acknowledgments

This section is always the most difficult part of a book to write. How can I thank every person who has impacted and influenced my thinking on this text? I am convinced we learn more by listening than by speaking, and I know many wonderful teachers who have given me a great deal of food for thought since I started writing this book.

I want to begin by thanking the teachers who took time out of their already packed schedules to try out ideas and listen to my thoughts. Those teachers and their students played a significant role in the creation of this text, and without them it wouldn't exist. Thanks especially to Lisa Carp, Andrea Continanzi, Marissa Hoff, Mary Lee, Jennifer Roberson, and Amanda Snow. Also, discussions I had with teachers I met through recent presentations at the Arkansas Reading Association Conference, the International Reading Association Conference, and the Reading Council of Greater Winnipeg have taught me a great deal.

In addition, I learn daily from my students and value their thoughts and feedback. Amanda Kane, J. William Lee, and Lisa Kuan have been especially helpful with their scientific knowledge, and I know their future and the future of our children are bright when educators such as these are guiding learning.

Thanks as well to Katherine Bryant for all of her hard work. She gave me a chance to write this book, and for that I will always be grateful. Her feedback was specific, fast, and brilliant. Her fantastic suggestions moved me from my initial idea for the text to a book that will help many science teachers in the classroom.

Colleagues both past and present, including Dan Ouzts, Lane Roy Gauthier, John Beach, Della Dekay, and others, helped me to keep my sanity as I navigated speaking and writing deadlines. Their sense of humor and friendship are always greatly appreciated.

Also, I thank my son, Ashenafi. Many hours were spent working on this project instead of watching *Sid the Science Kid*, conducting science experiments, and visiting the children's museum. A book is not created in isolation, and I know it takes away quality time from those close to us to get things done.

Finally, I thank the readers of this book. My hope is that by asking questions, engaging with ideas, and thinking about information contained within the pages of this book, we can continue to facilitate and strengthen connections between science and literacy. Please take the time to let me know your thoughts and suggestions on ideas shared in this book. In that way we can all continue to learn.

Introduction

With the large amount of scientific information we expect our students to learn today, we already struggle to find enough minutes in the classroom to develop that knowledge. Then just when we feel like we don't have an extra minute to spare, we have the additional pressure to include literacy skills. But the truth is, literacy skills aren't add-ons to the science class, put there because others expect us to include reading and writing in the classroom because of standards or curriculum frameworks. Instead, these skills are critical parts of science instruction. By enabling our students to comprehend a variety of scientific texts and communicate scientific understanding, we open doors for them. We know that career opportunities are plentiful in STEM (science, technology, engineering, and mathematics) fields, but beyond that, we want all students to grasp scientific content in order to better understand the world around them. Although there is no way we can teach students all of the scientific content they must know, we can teach them how to access that content so that they can continue to learn long after they walk out the doors of our classrooms.

I hope that you view this book as an invitation to reflect on how science and literacy can connect in your classroom. Whether you are just beginning your teaching journey or have many years of teaching experience, the ideas, suggestions, and activities within the pages you will read are meant to serve as the foundation upon which you can create important connections between science and literacy. These connections, which help students to think, read, and write like scientists, are the disciplinary literacy skills necessary to strengthen their scientific knowledge. Science requires specialized literacy demands, and these demands serve as the basis for this book.

About This Book

Throughout the book, you'll find brief "Think About It" and "Take Action" sections that will encourage you to reflect on your own teaching and try some new ideas. If you're reading the text alone, these sections will provide opportunities to gather your thoughts and apply ideas found within the text. They can also serve as good discussion starters if you're reading the book as part of a study group or book club.

The five chapters of this book include student examples from various grade levels and practical activities that you can use and modify to meet the needs of your students. You will also find that many of the activities involve collaboration among students. This type of collaboration reflects the learning that takes place in real life. Seldom do scientists work in isolation as they seek answers to scientific questions and find ways to effectively communicate their findings. Therefore, we need to encourage this type of collaboration in our classrooms.

Chapter 1 starts by answering the question, Why do we need to teach literacy skills in our science classes? It then lays out eight challenges we face in the science classroom, what those challenges mean for our teaching, and how they also give rise to important opportunities to engage students as scientific thinkers.

Chapter 2 takes a closer look at the texts we use in our classrooms. The most widely used text in the science classroom is the science textbook, but there are many other forms of text that we can integrate into our classrooms to strengthen scientific understanding. While the emphasis in education is clearly on informational text, these texts range from trade books to electronic texts and even to local texts. This chapter not only examines the types of text we might use but also looks at suggestions for locating and selecting the texts.

Developing vocabulary knowledge is the focus of Chapter 3. Vocabulary is important so that students can not only comprehend text that they hear or read but also accurately communicate scientific information. The chapter begins with ideas for determining the science terms students need to learn. Obviously our students encounter many unknown words, so we have to know how to determine which of those words deserve our time and focus. Not all terms are best taught in the same manner, so this chapter also takes a look at a variety of practical ideas for developing various types of vocabulary, and how we can engage students by giving them choice in the vocabulary they learn and broadening their exposure to a wide range of scientific terms.

Reading scientific text does our students no good if they can't comprehend it, so I've dedicated all of Chapter 4 to building comprehension skills. In order for comprehension to occur, our students must develop what I refer to as *text flexibility*: the ability to recognize that different types of text need different approaches. Students must be taught the best way to approach scientific text as opposed to other types of text with which they may be more familiar. Informational text has many unique features, and before students can focus on the content of a scientific text, they must learn to navigate those features. Our students must not only understand a text's content but also synthesize information they read in multiple sources, support their opinions with specific textual references, and realize the important role the author's purpose plays in a text's creation.

As students learn to comprehend scientific text, we can't forget about the importance of images. Images play a very important role in scientific text, so these images are the focus of Chapter 5. While many of our students may *see* images, do they really *look* at them? Can they shift between reading text and viewing images and synthesize the information both provide? Without truly analyzing and understanding images, our students may not understand scientific content. This chapter provides a close examination of various types of images students encounter in science.

Final Thoughts

Although this book is divided neatly into five chapters, we all know that literacy skills and life in general are messy. The content from every chapter spills out into other chapters. We need to use the understanding of diverse texts we develop in Chapter 2 as we read and reflect on the content in Chapters 3 through 5. Also, knowledge of images, as discussed in Chapter 5, is an integral part of students' comprehension of scientific text, detailed in Chapter 4. We must continually remember that our overall goal is to develop students who can access scientific content.

My greatest hope is to hear from teachers who write and highlight all over their copies of this text. That is when I will really feel like I am providing some assistance in the important process of connecting science and literacy. Grab a marker or highlighter, or turn on your e-book reader, and start reading this text. Even better, grab a few other colleagues and have a book club where you can share ideas that you try and discuss how you can modify some of the suggestions in this text to better fit your students' needs. We must look at literacy skills not as a time stealer that uses up precious minutes during the teaching of science but rather as something that complements the science curriculum. We need both literacy and science skills to create scientists in our classrooms and to prepare our students for the future challenges they will meet. Now, it's time to get started.

1

Making the Science–Literacy Connection

H as there ever been a better time to teach science? While the job is far from easy because of increasing district expectations, changing standards, and the feeling that there is never enough time in the day, it's an exciting and challenging time for teachers who dedicate their lives to helping students strengthen their scientific knowledge. Right now, you can open almost any educational journal or newspaper, turn on your computer, or watch the feeds in social media and realize that more and more attention is being drawn to the field of science and the methods through which the content is taught.

Nobody can deny that teachers of science are passionate about their content. This passion led you to choose to become science teachers so that you can pass on your love of science to your students. Your challenge is taking your passion and knowledge and using it to create students who are passionate and knowledgeable about the field of science. It isn't easy, and there are many challenges you face in developing your students' scientific knowledge. However, there is one common link that can help you meet these challenges: literacy.

Rethinking the Science–Literacy Relationship

In order to gain scientific knowledge, our students must be able to understand scientific material. This requires our students to possess the literacy skills necessary to read, view, and articulate scientific thoughts. Most of us are familiar with the phrase *content area literacy*. Many of us took a content literacy course in order to become a teacher. Often the content in a class such as this focuses on specific strategies that can help students understand content area material. Whether planning to teach math, science, or social studies, everyone sits together to learn how to use SQ3R (Robinson 1946), KWL (Ogle 1986), and other popular content area strategies with future students. Then future teachers walk out of the classroom with notebook pages or word documents full of strategies to use in lessons.

If you are like me, and took a class similar to this, the confidence didn't last long. In fact, by the time I could locate the well-worn notebooks during my first year of teaching or find the file folders containing the notes or locate electronic files that were lost in computer crashes or moves, it was apparent that the information from that class was not helping my teaching of science as much as I was hoping. We get frustrated because we work long hours each day to help our students access scientific material, and yet many of our students continue to struggle with the scientific texts we want them to read.

We Must Focus on Scientific Literacy Skills

Instead of looking at everything with a broad lens, we need to look more closely at the materials, demands, and requirements for our own content area. Research by Shanahan and Shanahan (2008) emphasizes that each content area has unique literacy demands, known as disciplinary literacy skills, and it is through the development of these important skills that our students learn to read, write, and think like historians, scientists, and mathematicians. In particular, Shanahan and Shanahan list these literacy skills specific to scientists:

» Scientists must be able to read and comprehend a wide variety of texts, and often they must also be able to examine and compare information from multiple sources on the same topic.

» Scientists must not only possess a large scientific vocabulary but also know how to determine the meaning of new words they encounter in scientific text.

» Scientists must be able to not only understand images but also shift their attention from printed text to images and back to printed text in order to comprehend text.

Of course even if our students do not choose to pursue scientific fields, they still need to develop these disciplinary literacy skills in science so that they will be able to make educated decisions and be contributing members of society. As adults, we often have to make decisions regarding the type of medical treatment we or a loved one might need. We also need to be advocates for practices that can positively influence our neighborhoods and families. We debate whether fluoride should be added to water or whether a factory might be impacting cancer rates in our communities. The only way we can read about, research, and intelligently respond to these issues is through the development of these disciplinary literacy skills. These skills are important to all of our students.

Why Is This Our Job? Why Are We Perfect for the Job?

As teachers of science, we are ideal for teaching the literacy skills our students need to understand science. We aren't teaching students to read for the sake of learning to read but rather helping them to develop the specific types of literacy skills they need to not only learn scientific information but also be

THINK ABOUT **Life as a Scientist**

What types of text must a scientist read as part of a scientific career?

Can you think of any distinct differences between the types of reading scientists do and those of historians or mathematicians? Are the types of text a scientist encounters present in your classroom? How does your science classroom prepare students to think, read, and write like scientists?

able to ultimately think and read about science topics independently. It seems more appropriate to look at ourselves as *disciplinary literacy experts*. We must know the specific literacy skills necessary for students to comprehend scientific information and articulate their understanding. For us, that means we need to continually think about the skills necessary to create scientists in our classroom and know how we can best develop those skills.

As science teachers, our goal is to develop students who can understand and evaluate sources of scientific information. Not only must students be able to comprehend what the author is stating in the scientific text, but they must also be able to realize that all text is not created equal, and not all information they read is accurate. They must be aware of the importance of examining multiple sources of information on a scientific topic and understand that an author may have had a reason for presenting information in the way that it is shared. Our students must use their knowledge of images and vocabulary in order to gain meaning from the text.

We also want our students to develop the skills and strategies necessary to ultimately be able to increase and deepen their scientific knowledge independently. This requires putting the appropriate scaffolds in place to enable our students to develop these literacy skills. Therefore, this teaching must occur while students are learning scientific information. The integration of literacy and science is a necessary part of our classrooms.

The Standards Actually Support Our Goal

I'm sure you have heard a lot about the English Language Arts Common Core State Standards (ELA CCSS) and the Next Generation Science Standards (NGSS). The ELA CCSS for grades 6–12 include an entire section of standards specifically relating to science and technical subjects. These standards emphasize developing academic vocabulary, citing evidence from text, and using content-rich nonfiction. The NGSS also expect students to use literacy skills as they compare and contrast multiple texts, develop argumentation skills, analyze and interpret data, and evaluate information and communicate it.

While these standards may feel overwhelming when we add them to our already full plates, these literacy-focused standards actually will help us to strengthen our students' scientific knowledge. Obviously, hands-on experiences must continue to play a central role in our classrooms as students develop

THINK ABOUT Addressing Our Challenges
• •
What do you believe are the most challenging aspects of scientific knowledge that may be addressed through literacy instruction? Are students struggling with scientific vocabulary, images, overall comprehension of information? What have you tried in the past to help students deal with the challenges? How did those strategies work?

scientific knowledge. However, at the same time we realize that when students struggle with scientific text or vocabulary demands, it can negatively impact the amount of scientific learning they gain from these experiences. How can our students synthesize the results of their scientific experiments with other written research if they don't have access to scientific text because of a lack of disciplinary literacy skills? What if our students cannot articulate their findings to others because of an inability to visually represent their findings or unfamiliarity with specific vocabulary terms? Our students need these literacy skills to support the knowledge they gain through engaging science experiences we provide for them, and the current standards support the need for that knowledge.

Embracing the Challenges and Opportunities of Science and Literacy

Integrating science and literacy is challenging, but challenges often strengthen learning by the opportunities they provide. Let's take a look at some of the challenges we may face in our science classrooms and see what each of these challenges means for us as science teachers. As you look at each of these challenges, you can also think about the opportunities each of them provides you as a science educator. While I discuss the challenges briefly below, the rest of this book will help you to not only meet these challenges but also take advantage of the opportunities they provide.

Students' Science Background

To begin with, we have to think about what students know and understand about science when they walk through our classroom doors. Unfortunately, there are a lot of grim statistics regarding the amount of time that students actually engage with science in elementary classrooms. In some classrooms it is no more than sixteen minutes per day (Winters Keegan 2006). That is less than the amount of time most students spend in elementary classrooms listening to announcements or transitioning from content area to content area during each week of school. It clearly isn't enough time to focus on science.

While we'd love to see this change, and see elementary teachers spend more time on science, the reality is that our middle school students may not have the scientific background we expect them to have when they walk through our classroom doors. If they aren't passionate about science, it may not be from a lack of interest but merely from minimal exposure. Therefore, the experiences we provide for our students are pivotal in influencing their views of the scientific field.

What Does This Mean for You?

We can't assume our students have an adequate scientific background to use the classroom textbook and to understand the vocabulary we use in our science classrooms, so we need to help build that background. We can do this by incorporating a wide variety of texts, such as online texts, articles, and trade books, into our lessons. If we're required to use a textbook, we can supplement it with other texts to help those students who may need to increase their background knowledge so that they can understand the science topics we teach. By recognizing this need, we can successfully build our students' interest in and passion for science. This interest is the necessary foundation for supporting and strengthening their scientific knowledge base. By taking into consideration our students' level of scientific knowledge and expanding the texts and strategies with which we approach our students' learning, we can develop scientifically knowledgeable students.

Diverse Needs

Our science classrooms are becoming more ethnically and culturally diverse. Students bring to our classrooms unique experiences, perspectives, and backgrounds. Our challenge is meeting all of their needs. Diversity is a good thing.

There is no doubt about that. However, this diversity is also a challenge because we want all of our students to be successful in strengthening their level of scientific knowledge.

What Does This Mean for You?

To reach all of our students, we need to familiarize ourselves with a wide range of strategies so that not just high-achieving students develop scientific skills. We must modify strategies and activities so that all students can reach their potential, including ELL students and those who struggle with reading or have other learning challenges. We can encourage our students to both develop and represent their knowledge through a variety of ways. Reading multimodal texts, working with peers, and using images can help students understand the science content. Our ultimate goal is for all students to be able to independently use a variety of strategies to gain scientific knowledge from texts and other sources, drawing on their unique backgrounds and strengths as they do so.

Prior Reading Experiences

Many of our students may not be reading a wide variety of informational texts either inside or outside of school. Outside of school, they may read about favorite television shows, fictional stories, and even graphic novels. Inside the English language arts classroom, the focus is often on fictional stories or hybrid texts (those stories that weave fiction and fact). Therefore, our students may not have the experience necessary to understand the informational science texts we present them.

What Does This Mean for You?

We must understand informational texts and the unique demands they present. While we will look more closely at informational texts in Chapter 2, let's briefly look at how informational texts differ from other types of text with which our students may be more familiar: the use of informational text features (e.g., headings, table of content, fonts), the amount of content presented, and the fact that students must read informational texts primarily to gain information rather than read for pleasure, as they often do when reading narrative text. We have to help students recognize the organizational structure of the diverse texts and develop their ability to read, write, and interact with a wide range of tools and media. Even students whom we may typically classify as *good* readers can have difficulty understanding scientific material if they are unfamiliar with a specific type of text. By focusing our efforts on helping students understand the unique demands of a wide variety of scientific texts, we are providing opportunities for them to critically read and understand texts they will encounter in science—skills that are imperative if they are to independently engage with information they encounter in scientific texts.

Active Involvement

We all know that research supports less rote memorization of science facts and the creation of more student knowledge through inquiry-based approaches (Conderman and Woods 2008). This inquiry learning requires students to be actively engaged with scientific material. As teachers of science, we thrive on providing students with hands-on experiments. So why is the expectation of active involvement in science instruction a challenge? Well, let's think about the amount of time our students spend outside of school watching YouTube videos, chatting on social media, or playing games. In fact, the amount of screen time students have outside of class is a constant source of discussion. These types of experiences often are passive. Students don't have to spend a great deal of time thinking about what they are doing. However, today's students need to be actively playing a part in their learning and constantly thinking about what is occurring in the science classroom. While our students may appear to be actively participating in science experiments and reading, are they thinking about what is occurring and why, or are they passive spectators?

What Does This Mean for You?

We can actively engage our students with scientific information by making connections between their personal and prior experiences and what is occurring in the science classroom. We can also involve them with selecting vocabulary terms to learn and choosing scientific texts they want to examine. When they seek out diverse texts on the topic to see what others say about the topic, they are actively engaged with the content. Scientific knowledge is dynamic and requires investigation. We must require that our students scrutinize information, consider sources, and question how information on a topic is changing or may change as they gain more information.

Our students must challenge each other and ask questions about scientific information they are processing. Through reading both traditional and digital text, articulating their opinions on the topics and text, and creating questions, students realize that their opinions and views play a role in the classroom, and they can also challenge their own and other students' thinking instead of assuming all information they read is factual.

While our students may spend quite a bit of time outside our classrooms passively participating in life experiences, we need to ensure that our science classrooms are student-centered and less teacher-driven. Since students actively contribute in a student-centered classroom, this type of climate also requires much more group interaction. While we already have our students complete experiments in groups or through hands-on activities, we have to encourage active student engagement in *all* aspects of the science classroom.

Science Textbooks

As teachers of science, many of us are required to use a particular textbook. These textbooks are mass-produced to cover certain scientific content regardless of students' needs. Frequently they are difficult for students to read and understand.

What Does This Mean for You?

We don't have to abandon our textbooks, but we definitely want to see them as only one source of information. Diverse texts include both print and digital texts, such as science journals, instructions for science experiments, research articles, and other types of print. Our science classrooms provide an opportunity to introduce our students to these many different types of scientific writing, which they will continue to encounter throughout their lives whether they become scientists or not, and to different perspectives about scientific issues.

Vocabulary Demands

When I ask teachers what makes science content challenging, vocabulary is often one of the first things they mention. According to Fang (2004), science is more lexically dense than many content areas. In fact, the ratio of content words to general words is higher in science than in social studies or math. When we add this lexical density to some of the prior challenges, such as diverse student backgrounds and limited experience with science content, vocabulary can present a huge issue in our classrooms and keep our students from becoming knowledgeable about science.

What Does This Mean for You?

Many of the new science terms our students encounter are technical words they do not see in other content areas. We have to help our students build that academic vocabulary. Many other vocabulary words our students encounter in our science classrooms are multi-meaning terms and may have a different meaning in science than in everyday speech. These multi-meaning terms create confusion for our students, especially for ELLs. Also, some terms are not science specific but play a key role in accessing science content, such as *synthesize*, *replicate*, and *evaluate*. Mastering both the scientific vocabulary and strategies for figuring out unfamiliar terms will serve students well in our classes and in their future learning.

Extensive Use of Images

Given that many of our students spend a great deal of their hours outside of class on screen time, they are undoubtedly exposed to a lot of images. But they may be passive consumers of images; they may not actually think about what they are viewing in the way that they must think about images they encounter in science. The challenge isn't the number of images our students will encounter in our science classrooms but rather how we expect them to engage with the images.

What Does This Mean for You?

Often science texts contain graphs, video links, diagrams, and other types of images. In order to understand science content, students must move back and forth between images and words to gain the text's meaning. Therefore, we must guide our students in understanding the important role images play in science

FIND OUT HOW STUDENTS VIEW SCIENCE AND SCIENCE TEXT

Have students brainstorm their thoughts on their experiences with science and science classes. Is there anything that makes science really difficult for them? What activities are often part of science class? Are there specific experiences that stand out? What do they especially like or dislike about science class? How do they gain scientific information outside of class?

Collect and read through students' thoughts, looking for patterns within the class responses. What type of texts do they discuss, if any? Is science a topic to experience or facts to memorize? Do students mention vocabulary or difficult words in science? Do they talk about graphs, charts, or other images?

This brief activity can reveal student perceptions and misconceptions about science. Perhaps they see the textbook or any text as *the* source of information. Our students may see questions or discussion merely as a way to find out if they know a specific answer instead of a way to further their scientific understanding. Do any of them mention the importance of science to the world outside the classroom? Perhaps many of our students struggle with new words they encounter in science.

After reading through student comments, discuss the results with students and talk about goals for the class. After trying some of the ideas in this book, ask students to write their beliefs about science again and see if anything has changed in their responses. ✱

text and then assist them in navigating images so that they can use the information they gain from the images to strengthen their scientific knowledge. Students must also critically examine images just as they do the printed word. We can provide them the opportunities to practice these crucial skills.

Overwhelming Amount of Scientific Information

With the click of a computer key, our students can view an overwhelming amount of scientific information, but there is no guarantee that they are critical consumers of the information they encounter. We may find that our students merely soak in what they find on the Internet without giving a lot of thought to whether the information is accurate or not.

What Does This Mean for You?

We must teach students to question what they read now more than ever before. While the Internet requires additional literacy skills that are not necessary with reading traditional text, such as the ability to search and navigate websites, a lot of the literacy skills necessary for students to comprehend digital resources are basic literacy skills we all need to focus on with our students. Some in the educational field raise the concern that we often don't ask students to question the information they encounter in text, *period* (Thompson 2011). So while technology helps to remind us that students must be critical of what they read, this is an important skill for all scientific information students encounter, regardless of the source.

Before Moving On

As you think about the eight challenges in this chapter, you'll see a common thread that ties the challenges together. That thread is literacy. As teachers of science, we must use literacy skills to help meet our students' diverse needs and to deepen their scientific understanding. Our students will be able to better access science information if we engage them with diverse texts, work on building scientific vocabulary, focus on comprehension, and provide them with the knowledge necessary to intelligently engage with images in the science classroom. The standards we strive to meet acknowledge that thread and support our mission for strengthening our students' science knowledge through addressing literacy skills. The remaining chapters in this book will help you to meet these challenges and use literacy skills to strengthen your students' science knowledge. We'll begin in Chapter 2 by looking at the scientific texts we use.

2

· · · · · · · · · · · · ·

Expanding Our Vision of Scientific Texts

As I take a peek in Maria's fourth-grade science classroom, students are huddled together in small groups, looking at the rain forests they created in soda bottles the week prior. They press their faces close to the bottles, and I can hear the enthusiasm in their voices as they talk about what they see. After about ten minutes, Maria asks the groups to take turns sharing what they have noticed. As students share ideas, she ties their comments back into a recently read textbook chapter on habitats.

Maria then encourages her students to work in groups to brainstorm questions they still have about rain forests. What else would they like to know? Each group quickly selects a recorder to jot down the group's ideas on a large sheet of paper. As I quietly walk around the room, I glance over the shoulders of students sprawled out on the floor, busily writing with brightly colored markers on chart paper. Right away it is evident that several groups want to know more about how changes in rain forests affect the rest of the world. Others question how rain forests have changed over time.

Fifteen minutes later, the groups are finished writing their questions. Maria asks each of the groups to share its thoughts with the rest of the class. As the students share their questions, Maria encourages each group to select one question on its sheet to research, and the students talk about where they might find answers. After selecting the question, some students decide to explore a new science website they recently learned about in class, while another group wants to take a closer look at trade books and magazines on rain forests in the classroom library. Maria has students write down their chosen questions in their science notebooks so that they can remember their research purpose. She asks them to locate three to five facts that provide information for their question and reminds them that it's important to cite their sources. Later in the week, the class will gather together to share the groups' findings.

Ensuring Text Diversity in the Classroom

As teachers, we know that our students need to be exposed to a wide variety of text in the science classroom, just as Maria's students were. In fact, the ELA CCSS and the NGSS require students to be able to use multiple texts to gain information. In order to meet the goals of the NGSS *Framework for K–12 Science Education*, students must engage with media reports of science, a variety of text features (e.g., graphs, tables, and other images), and both print and electronic material. However, whether or not our classrooms focus on these standards, we want our students to be well prepared so that they can independently engage with texts in order to gain scientific understanding later in life. Therefore, we must intelligently select and use diverse texts with the students in our classrooms. By incorporating diverse texts into our hands-on, inquiry-based science lessons, we can expand our students' view of "text" and enable them to develop a deeper knowledge of science content.

Why Not Just Use the Textbook?

Let's reflect on the role the textbook played in Maria's lesson and the role it plays in our own science classrooms. While Maria used the district-required science textbook, it is evident that she viewed it as only one source of information, not as *the* source of information. By doing so, she expanded her students' understanding of rain forests, encouraged the use of multiple texts, and showed students real-world ways in which adults gather information.

Research shows that the textbook plays a major role in many classrooms (Weiss and Pasley 2004), and this is especially true for fourth- through sixth-grade classrooms (Henke, Chen, and Goldman 1999). But many of us have heard complaints about textbooks or experienced our own frustrations firsthand when using them in the science classroom. Textbooks are designed to convey information, and yet they aren't the type of text most students will read at night under the covers with a flashlight or view on vacation with an e-reader. Not only are they mass-produced for large numbers of students who may have little in common, but because of the high cost of textbooks, they are used for many years in a district. While teachers, or a committee of teachers, in a school district often have the opportunity to vote on the textbook they would prefer to use, that doesn't necessarily mean it will be the one the school district adopts.

The bottom line is that textbooks assume a certain level of knowledge from the readers because textbooks aren't selected with specific students in mind. Also, because one textbook must cover a wide range of material, breadth of content coverage is often more typical than depth. It is clear that textbook publishers are able to give limited coverage to many important concepts in science textbooks (see, e.g., Decker, Summers, and Barrow 2007). The content that is present in the science texts is also a concern for many educators. Along with containing stereotypical images (Good, Woodzicka, and Wingfield 2010; Mattox 2008), the material is often presented in a dull manner (Ogan-Bekiroglu

THINK ABOUT the Science Textbook

Take a minute and think about some concerns you have with your students' science textbook. What specific aspects of the book create issues for your students? Is it visually engaging or unappealing? Does it cover a great deal of material but have very little depth?

Now think about other types of text that might be better suited to meet students' needs while diminishing some of those concerns. Reflect back on your ideas as you read through the rest of this chapter.

2007). However, perhaps the greatest concern is the adoption process of text-books. Textbook publishing is a business, and an extremely lucrative one at that. Therefore, science textbook publishers can be pressured by small influential groups to present information in such a way that their textbook is more apt to be adopted by states. This is especially true in states that have a statewide adoption process, removing the decision-making process from individual districts. For example, information pertaining to controversial topics (e.g., homosexuality, reproduction, sexually transmitted diseases) can be glossed over, slanted to reflect a certain perspective, or even omitted (Wiley and Barr 2007). While many of us may find these concerns alarming, the question becomes, What can we do about these concerns? We must ensure that the textbook is one of many types of text students encounter in our classrooms.

Broadening Our Text Use: Trade Books

Trade books are the books we find in libraries or bookstores, and for many reasons they're great supplementary texts to use with students. Unlike textbooks, recently published trade books have up-to-date content, are usually written by real authors instead of textbook publishers, and are easily accessible.

While students need to experience science through inquiry-based lessons, trade books can serve as an excellent way to support, reinforce, and extend our lessons (Morrison and Young 2008). Trade books expose students to scientific findings and places they can't explore within the classroom. It isn't realistic for us to fly our students through the solar system or take an actual look inside the human brain, but trade books can help us do that.

Types of Trade Books: Format

Trade books are often categorized as either chapter books or picture books according to their format. While chapter books tend to be rather lengthy, picture books use pictures (e.g., illustrations and photographs) as much as words to convey meaning. Picture books are often associated with very young learners, but that view is too limiting. Picture books can be very useful for all grade levels because they can be used to model a strategy or share information more quickly than a chapter book.

For example, many of our students may read a chapter book such as Katherine Applegate's 2013 Newbery Medal winner, *The One and Only Ivan* (2012), during language arts or English class. It is a fictional story based on the true story of a gorilla that was housed in a tiny cage in a shopping mall for over twenty years. Reading this fictional story provides the perfect opportunity to pair a nonfiction science picture book, such as Seymour Simon's *Gorillas* (2008), with it. Students can even locate newspaper articles about the original Ivan. As students research and learn about gorillas, they can compare the information in different texts and discuss the authors' purposes for the texts and how they may have influenced content presentation.

Other picture books, such as *Life-Size Zoo* (Komiya 2009), though suggested for younger students, can serve as excellent resources for older students. For example, students can analyze the unique way information is presented in the animal encyclopedia. What middle school student wouldn't enjoy learning that a capybara poops in the water or an elephant has forty thousand muscles in its trunk? After examining a text such as *Life-Size Zoo*, students can use the text to create an encyclopedia on another science topic. If we don't use picture books within our science classrooms, we are missing out on a valuable resource for our students.

Types of Trade Books: Content

Along with considering the format of trade books, we need to think about the content. While there are many types of trade books that might be tied into the science classroom or used to extend learning outside of the classroom, not all trade books are created equal. In fact, trade books vary widely. Let's think about the different types of science trade books we might use with our students. There are faction, poetry, and informational texts.

Faction

Just as the name implies, faction texts are a blend of facts and fiction (Avery 2003). While these books contain scientific facts, they tell a fictitious story. Although faction is a very popular type of story for primary-grade teachers to use with students, many of our fourth- and fifth-grade students, or older struggling readers, may also enjoy books such as Joanna Cole's Magic School Bus chapter books. Also, science fiction texts are a popular type of faction text for older students to read. Science fiction texts, which portray the future, are generally based on scientific principles but told in narrative form.

Faction, including science fiction, allows our students to stretch their imaginations and think about the possibilities that exist with science. However, faction is probably the most controversial of the three types of trade books mentioned. The issue is that younger children often have difficulty separating the facts from the fiction in faction, and they remember the story instead of the facts (Bamford, Kristo, and Lyons 2002). While our students are older, we may see the same issues that younger children experience with faction. Can students locate the factual information in the text? Will they remember the scientific principles discussed within the pages of the fictional story? Whether we choose to use faction in the classroom or not, students will encounter these texts in other settings. Faction, if we help students understand it, provides an opportunity to expand our students' schema for science text and to emphasize the importance of taking genre into consideration when we read text.

One teacher decided to use faction to reinforce her students' study of text structures in reading. She decided to use Cole's *Magic School Bus Inside the Human Body* (1990) because many students were familiar with the series but were less familiar with the term *faction*. As they began their discussion, they talked about how texts can contain not only a fictional story but also scientific facts. Students named other familiar books that contained facts and fiction, such as *Unsinkable*, the first book in Gordan Korman's Titanic trilogy (2011). The teacher discussed how as scientists and readers of text, they must be able to find the scientific facts in text and be able to separate fact from fiction. The students watched as the teacher modeled how to do this with the first few pages of the Cole book. Then she invited the students to join in and determine which parts of the book were scientific facts and which parts were fictional. As she read the book, she wrote a couple of examples in a T-chart on a large sheet of paper. The class completed the chart, and then students were asked to each create a T-chart with another faction text on their own. Figure 2.1 is the finished T-chart her class created.

The Magic School Bus: Inside the Human Body

Scientific Facts	Fiction
• most cells are so small that we can't see them without a microscope.	• At once we started shrinking and spinning through the air— Ms. Frizzle said we were inside a human body.
• Your body is made of many pieces called cells.	- ...bus turning round and round and digestive juice splashed on the windows
• Your tongue is covered with thousands of taste buds.	- Ms. Frizzle drove to the bottom of the stomach.
- The walls of the stomach moved in and out, churning and mashing the food into a thick liquid.	- We were swept out of the bus and into the bloodstream.
- The inner walls of the small intestine were covered with tiny "fingers" called villi.	
- Red blood cells carry oxygen from the lungs to all the cells of the body.	

◀ FIGURE 2.1

Poetry

Poetry is my favorite genre to use with science. First of all, poems are usually very short so they can be easily incorporated into almost any science lesson. This sharing can spark students' interest in a topic, encourage student writing on a topic, and provide students with an opportunity to view a topic in an entirely new way. We might not have the time to teach students all about the genre of poetry, but we can reinforce poetic elements and encourage students to appreciate another type of text while strengthening science content knowledge.

For example, Shields and Thompson's *Brainjuice: Science, Fresh Squeezed!* (2003) includes a variety of poems related to earth and space, life science, and chemistry. Consider introducing science topics by orally sharing and discussing poems such as the ones in this text with students. Since many of our students also grew up enjoying Scieszka's *Math Curse* (1995), you may want to share some of the poems found in *Science Verse* (2004), by the same author. Topics include everything from viruses to combustion reaction. Since the poems read better as songs, you can use some of the poems as models so students can create their own science chants or raps about science topics.

Informational Texts

Quality faction and poetry add educational value to our science content. The texts convey scientific information and expose our students to a wider range of genres. But if our goal is to create science-knowledgeable students in our classrooms, we can't do that by sharing only faction and poetry texts. Our students must also be exposed to a great deal of informational text. They need to see texts written to convey scientific explanations, experiments, and reports (Donovan and Smolkin 2001). Since informational texts are the most important for science classrooms, I'll focus on them for the rest of this chapter.

In the last ten to fifteen years, there has been a great deal of focus on the importance of informational text. A lot of this emphasis is due to the fact that Nell Duke (2000) published a large-scale, groundbreaking study showing that young children were exposed to only 3.6 minutes of informational text per day during whole-class language arts activities. When we look back on our own experience in the early grades, many of us will recall that we were fed a steady diet of wonderful fictional tales. However, the ELA Common Core State Standards require an increasing percentage of texts used in the classroom to be informational. This shift is occurring even in primary grades, but we must realize that many of our students may have much more experience with narrative than informational texts. This is important to note because informational texts have unique qualities of which our students must be aware.

Let's identify some of the common characteristics of informational text:

» **Author's Goal:** Informational books aren't written to entertain (even though high-quality informational text is engaging). The texts are written because the author wants the reader to learn information.

» **Language Use:** Often informational texts use generic nouns and present-tense verbs. A fictional story about astronauts might read similar to this: "Astronaut Dwight stepped into the rocket, excited to be one of the first astronauts to visit the new planet." An informational text would instead have language such as "This is the first space voyage for the astronaut. He carefully puts on his Advanced Crew Escape Suit (ACES), an important orange suit. The ACES is designed to protect him during the launch."

» **Text Features:** Features such as photographs, captions, highlighting, fonts, tables of contents, text boxes, graphs, and glossaries are important components of informational text. The features included in informational trade books vary, but through our careful selection of trade books, we can make sure that we expose our students to a wide range of features.

» **Style:** Scientists use a lot of technical vocabulary when they write reports or explanations. Directions for specific experiments and other types of scientific writing are often very succinct and to the point. Even persuasive pieces must be backed with factual information.

It is important to be aware of the diverse texts that can enhance our students' scientific learning, but how can we take that knowledge and fill our classrooms with quality text?

Finding and Choosing Trade Books

Although there are many science trade books available, choosing and locating them can be a challenge. Figure 2.2 provides a list of sources that identify outstanding science texts (in some cases, among other types of texts).

One of my favorite sources for identifying good science trade books is the Database of Award-Winning Children's Literature (www.dawcl.com), a website created by a librarian. The website allows a teacher to search over ten thousand texts through a variety of variables, such as age of reader, publication date (important to ensure up-to-date information), science topic, and awards won. You can also search for texts reflecting people of specific ethnicities or genders. This is important so that all students can see role models similar to themselves in science texts.

You can also find teachers discussing and recommending favorite science trade books on blogs, Pinterest boards, personal learning communities, and even in Twitter chats (see Appendix A for some specific recommendations). Figure 2.3 lists some popular authors of science trade books.

SOURCES FOR OUTSTANDING CHILDREN'S TRADE BOOKS

Young Adults' Choices Reading List: www.reading.org/Resources/Booklists /YoungAdultsChoices.aspx

Teachers' Choices Reading List: www.reading.org/Resources/Booklists /TeachersChoices.aspx

NCTE Orbis Pictus Award for Outstanding Nonfiction for Children: www.ncte .org/awards/orbispictus

NSTA Outstanding Science Trade Books for Students K–12: www.nsta.org /publications/ostb

Smithsonian's Great Science Books for the Little Ones: http://blogs.smithsonianmag .com/science/2010/12/great-science-books-for-the-little-ones/

Popular Science Book Reviews: www.popularscience.co.uk/?cat=10

◀ FIGURE 2.2

POPULAR AUTHORS OF SCIENCE TRADE BOOKS

David Adler	Joanna Cole	Sy Montgomery
Caroline Arnold	Sneed Collard	Dorothy Hinshaw Patent
Jim Arnosky	Nicola Davies	April Pulley Sayre
Molly Bang	Gail Gibbons	Elaine Scott
Melvin Berger	Steve Jenkins	Millicent Selsam
Nic Bishop	Patricia Lauber	Seymour Simon
Franklyn M. Branley	Bianca Lavies	Pam Turner
Loree Griffin Burns	David Macaulay	Janice VanCleave
Vicki Cobb	Sandra Markle	

◀ FIGURE 2.3

Selecting the Texts to Use

The next question is how to select the texts that best meet our content goals. Figure 2.4 contains qualities to consider when selecting science trade books.

The Science Trade Book Evaluation Guide, as seen in Figure 2.4, is available as a reproducible in Appendix B. This guide can help you analyze the five key aspects of science trade books. After using the guide a few times, you will begin to internalize its ideas, making it easier to evaluate texts you encounter. Let's take a closer look at each area of the Science Trade Book Evaluation Guide.

Science Content

In science texts, we need information to be accurate. Through science texts, students can not only learn scientific information but also develop scientific misconceptions (Rice 2002). Following are some key points to evaluate:

» Does the text mention experts the author consulted and contain background information on the author? If the author does not have experience directly related to the content discussed in the text, then it is important to be able to see that the author consulted experts while writing the text.

APPENDIX B   Science Trade Book Evaluation Guide

AREA OF FOCUS	NOTES

Science Content

- ○ Were experts consulted?
- ○ Does it include background info on author and/or illustrator?
- ○ Is there any misleading information?
- ○ Are the information and copyright current?
- ○ Is it free of stereotypes?

Images

- ○ Are the illustrations realistic?
- ○ Do the photographs support the text, and are they accompanied by credits?
- ○ Are the drawings accurate in scale?

Writing

- ○ Is it engaging for students?
- ○ Is there a logical presentation?
- ○ Does the text include precise scientific terminology?

Informational Text Features

- ○ Does it contain useful labels, captions, sidebars, and/or charts and keys?
- ○ Is there a useful table of contents and/ or glossary?
- ○ Does it use different typefaces for emphasis?

Overall Design

- ○ Are the layout and format appropriate?
- ○ Is it appealing to students?

◀ FIGURE 2.4

» Look at the copyright date to ensure that current information on the topic is being shared.

» While topics may not be discussed in great detail, it is important to ensure that simplification of the topic does not result in misleading information.

» Examine both text and images in science texts to ensure that ethnic, socioeconomic status, and gender stereotypes are not present. Science texts have had a history of reinforcing stereotypes, and we want to encourage all students to engage with science. While the current ratio of men to women graduating with bachelor's degrees in earth science are pretty equal, physical geology textbooks portray men as more than three times as likely as women to become geologists and Caucasians as fifteen times as likely as other ethnicities to be in the workforce (Mattox 2008). This is a problem because stereotypes found in science textbook images have been shown to influence science performance (Good, Woodzicka, and Wingfield 2010). Research found that female students comprehended more scientific information when the images in a text contained counter-stereotypes such as female scientists than when the images present within the same chunk of text were stereotypical.

Images

Images play an important role in science texts because they convey and extend information found in the written words. Any illustrations included in text should be realistic and accurate in scale so as not to present misconceptions. Also, if photographs are used, photo credits should be provided, and the photographs should support the text. Photo credits are important because just as we look for citations with text, we must know the origin of photographs. By having the citation, the reader knows that the person or persons listed are stating that that photograph is what it claims to be in the text.

Writing

While we want texts to use precise scientific terminology, we want to ensure that the writing isn't dry and boring. The author should have a lively voice and include numerous examples of concepts. The presentation of content is also important. Students will encounter difficulty with text if the author's thoughts are hard to follow. Through a logical presentation of concepts within the text, students should be able to learn about scientific facts and want to learn more on the topic.

Informational Text Features

Of course it's not realistic to expect every text to contain labels, captions, sidebars, charts and keys, and a variety of other textual features. However, it is important to note the features that are found within the texts we select so that we ensure we have texts in our classroom containing a variety of features.

Overall Design

Have you ever picked up a science text with unusually small typeface covering the pages from margin to margin and black-and-white images? It probably wasn't a text you eagerly wanted to read. Examining overall design requires us to look at the total text. Determine if the visual layout of the text will appeal to the students. Are the layout and design of the book such that kids will want to read it? Are they appropriate for the content? While not all scientific reading our students will encounter will be visually engaging, it is important for our students, who are still developing interests and learning to navigate complex text, to have the opportunity to interact with appealing books.

Sample Evaluation of a Text

Figure 2.5 shows the evaluation results of the trade book *Cicadas! Strange and Wonderful* (Pringle 2010). The analysis shows that the text has numerous strengths. If we are looking for a book on cicadas or know a student has a specific interest in insects, then this text might serve our purpose. The analysis reveals that there are several textual features that are not used in the text. We can use that information to help students understand texts and think about why the author may or may not have included certain elements. Would the features add to the text? With a text this short, perhaps a table of contents is not necessary. However, perhaps a glossary would be useful. Discussions like this help our students become critical consumers of text and draw their attention to qualities of text.

Science Trade Book Evaluation Guide

<u>Area of Focus</u>	<u>Notes</u>
Science Content	
Experts Consulted	*EXCELLENT* spec. experts at a lg. univ
Background Info. On Author/Illustrator	– au- exp as nature photographer + attempting to transplant cicadas.
No Misleading Information	
Current Information and Copyright	2010ⓒ
Free of Stereotypes	various ethnicities
Images	*DIVERSE*
Realistic Illustrations	maps – midwest, NE states flowchart of life cycle
Photographs Support Text/Credits	diagram of anatomy
Drawings Accurate in Scale	time line
Writing	
Engaging for Students	– ? at beg. of bk will engage ideas
Logical Presentation	additional sources of info provided
Precise Scientific Terminology	– compares to info kids know
Informational Text Features	
Labels, Captions, Sidebars, and/or Charts/Keys	– numerous fonts, colors, emphasis of subheadings & headings & / labels
Table of Contents and/or Glossary if Useful	NO glossary, t of c, or index (maybe not needed)
Typeface for Emphasis	
Overall Design	– visuals break up lg chunks of text
Appropriate Layout and Format	
Text has "kid" appeal (Moss 2003, page 41)	Biggest Consideration # of pgs & bk sz appealing Lg amt of text on some pgs will require - 3, talking through sharing other sources

◀ FIGURE 2.5

Also, the analysis reveals that on some pages there is still a great deal of text. With this knowledge, and given the fact that the book has many qualities we value, we can tailor our use of the book to fit our students' needs. Students with minimal background knowledge on the topic or who struggle with reading may need additional scaffolding throughout the text. We can skim through the book and determine areas where we might want to stop and assess student understanding, engage our students through content questions, and connect new information to that with which they are familiar.

Obtaining Trade Books

Now that you know what to look for in texts, you have to actually obtain the books. With school budgets tightening everywhere, finding the funds for trade books is difficult. Science trade books need to contain up-to-date information, so using old texts is not a good option. It may be easiest to get texts from libraries, eliminating the need to buy new books often.

However, there is a website, www.donorschoose.org, where teachers in public schools can apply for funds to purchase needed books and materials. Teachers write grants requesting the funds, and the grants can remain posted on the website for up to four months. Anyone can select and donate to projects they want to support. Donations as small as one dollar are encouraged. According to the site, approximately 70 percent of grants are funded.

TAKE
ACTION

CHECK OUT DAWCL

Using www.dawcl.com and the information in Figure 2.2 and Figure 2.3, determine five to ten trade books that might be used with a science topic you're planning to teach soon. Create a list of the texts, and try to locate them in local libraries. Then evaluate the texts you found according to the guide in Figure 2.4. If possible, work with another teacher so that you can discuss the results. Did your view of any of the texts change after using the evaluation guide?

How might the guide influence your future text selections? Are there new aspects of texts introduced on the guide that you hadn't previously considered when selecting trade books? *

Capitalizing on Local Text

There is another important type of text that costs almost nothing to produce, is readily accessible, and can be incredibly powerful when displayed in our science classrooms. Maloch, Hoffman, and Patterson (2004) refer to it as *local text*. While imported texts such as trade books and worksheets are brought into the classroom environment, local text is created by those within the classroom community. While publisher-created materials and posters we get from national conferences and companies can create a print-rich environment in our science classroom, local texts are more personally meaningful to the students within the classroom community than imported texts, and they serve to reinforce the learning that is taking place. Local text is also inexpensive and readily available, and can be quickly and easily changed whenever science topics change. It provides yet another opportunity to create a print-rich environment.

Two Types of Local Text

There are two categories of local text that can be found in a classroom. The categories aren't determined by the end project (e.g., chart, group-created posters) but rather the manner in which our students engage with the text.

Local Text That Showcases Culminating Experiences

The first type of local text displays students' understanding of a concept. Examples include completed student projects and papers displayed for others to see. Many teachers already have this type of local text in the classroom. As students create this type of local text, they develop a deeper understanding of the scientific content, and they enjoy seeing the results of their work. Often this type of text can be created by students in small groups so that students have the added benefit of engaging with others in their class as they work. Through social interaction, or discussion with classmates in their group, students are able to expand their own scientific vocabulary and prior knowledge. By asking students to explain their work as they share their finished projects with others, and to answer questions, we encourage them to have a deep understanding of the content.

CONSIDER WRITING A GRANT

TAKE ACTION

If you could get money to enrich your science lessons, how would you use that money? What experiences and texts are your students lacking that would be attainable with that additional money?

Draft a small grant for science trade books or other forms of text you would like to get funded. Articulate the important role the texts will have in your science classroom, the exact types of books needed, and the amount of money needed to purchase them. If possible, get feedback on your proposal from other teachers in order to refine it. Consider seeking the approval of your department chair and/or principal so that you can submit it to www.donorschoose.org or a local agency that funds grants. ✱

One teacher, working toward the goal of having students understand features and changes in Earth's land and oceans, realized that her students were having difficulty understanding underwater landforms and what they looked like (a new topic for fifth graders). She showed the class a variety of images, both three-dimensional and linear, on the Internet. The class also created a 3-D model of the ocean floor. Then the class was divided into teams consisting of five to six students that each created a mural to illustrate the landforms. (See Figure 2.6.)

Students not only reinforced their knowledge of continental and oceanic landforms as they created their murals but also created local texts, which the

◀ FIGURE 2.6

teacher then displayed. The murals served to facilitate discussion among students as they viewed other groups' illustrations. Labeling the murals reinforced academic and domain-specific terms students would continue to encounter in class.

Local Text That Serves as an Ongoing, Interactive Part of Our Lessons

The second type of local text is text that we continually refer back to as our lessons progress. An important characteristic that sets this type of local text apart from the other type of local text is that students must continually engage with the text in order to continue to create it. Specific examples include charts, diagrams, and even science word walls.

As teachers, we should add to and modify this type of local text as the year progresses. For example, if you are beginning a unit on light, groups of students can create a very basic diagram or illustration showing how light behaves. As experiments are conducted, groups of students can modify or redesign their diagrams to illustrate how various wavelengths behave. These changes in the images will clear up misconceptions, include specific vocabulary terms they are learning relative to the topic, and enable students to more effectively share knowledge through images. During the unit, draw attention to the local text you've displayed so students can connect their prior learning with information they are currently learning.

If students are studying space, you might create a large mural on the wall with a simple outline of planets on it. As students gain more and more information about the solar system, they may engage with the mural by coloring

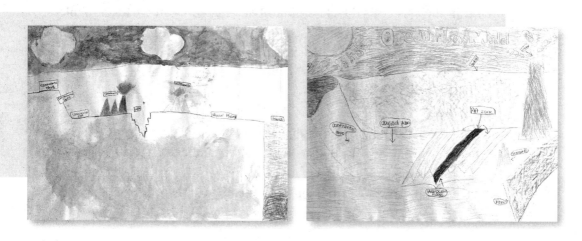

planets specific colors, adding rings, or moving their location on the mural. When students have a better understanding of distance between planets, the class may come up with a way to show the distance so that the planets are an accurate distance from each other on the mural.

Figure 2.7 is an example of this type of local text and represents a brainstorming chart one teacher hung in her classroom. After the chart was displayed, the class brainstormed terms pertaining to weathering that began with specific letters of the alphabet. As students contributed terms, the class discussed each term to ensure that the students had an understanding of the term and it was in their speaking vocabulary.

Through this brainstorming chart, the teacher was able to build academic vocabulary related to the topic the students were studying. Then as a class, students could continue to add on new words they encountered, thought were important, or were curious to learn. This type of local text is especially valuable because it continues to grow and change with the students. It evolves along with them. Since there is continual interaction with the chart, it remains a point of interest in the classroom.

We can also use labels in the classroom to create this type of text. Think about a science lesson on simple machines. What types of text might students create that could be displayed in the classroom? If the students look for simple machines in the classroom, they can write the type of simple machine on a strip of paper and label their findings. They can tape a small sheet of paper with the words *wheel and axle* written on it above the doorknob, the word *pulleys* by the cord on the blinds, *screw* next to the pencil sharpener, and *lever* by the broom in the corner of the classroom. Also, students can create a simple machine and then draw a diagram to scale of their creation on a sheet of graph paper. Perhaps the students look for examples of simple machines outside of class, take photographs of them, and add their findings to a word wall in the classroom.

One classroom teacher incorporated this type of local text into her classroom after a field trip to learn more about ecosystems. As part of this experience, her students were exposed to the terms *abiotic* and *biotic*. After returning to class, the class discussed whether items were abiotic or biotic. Then the teacher gave the students labels and tape and encouraged them to label items in the classroom.

Landforms and Oceans

A abyssal plains	B beach, **bay**	C constructive continental shelf canyon continental slope current	D destructive **deposition, delta**
E erosion earth quake	F floodplain flood	G glacier	H hill
I islands	J	K	L **land slides** landform
M mesa meander mid-ocean ridge mountain	N natural disasters	O oasis, ocean ocean basin	P plain plateau
Q	R rift zone rift	S seamount	T trench tributary
U underwater	V valley volcano volcanic eruption volcanic island	W weathering wave	X
Y	Z		

◀ FIGURE 2.7

We can also use this type of local text to strengthen student knowledge of scientists who have contributed to the topics they are studying. Select a few important people associated with a given topic. Be sure to include both males and females in the field as well as a variety of ethnicities. Then place an illustration or photo of each person on the wall. Outside of class, students can research the people and jot down important facts. During a few minutes in class, students can share additional information they learned about the scientists outside of class and add their note cards to the illustrations. As students study new scientific concepts, you can ask students how the current topic might tie to a specific person on the wall. This brief discussion can serve as an opportunity for students to compare and contrast information, to reflect back on prior learning, and to reinforce their current science learning.

The Value of Local Text

While many people may associate a print-rich environment with very young students, this type of environmental print provides reinforcement of scientific content for our older students. For English language learners, who need additional reinforcement of concepts and technical terms, this type of text can be invaluable. Furthermore, students create the text, so there is a sense of authorship. If there are student-created diagrams displayed in the room and trade books on simple machines in the class library, we all know that students will be much more eager to have visitors see the local text they created than the trade books.

It is important that all students be represented in the local text on display. Even students who may not be as scientifically knowledgeable as others can successfully create something of value to display, and group work can be an important part of local text. We want everyone's voice to be valued and for all students to have an opportunity to participate. Talk with students and engage them in conversations about local text. What type of text is valuable to display in the classroom? What purposes can it serve? Word walls and labels can reinforce new terms. Student-created images and writing will enable them to see growth in their skills. Group or whole-class activities, such as large sheets of paper containing brainstormed ideas or opinions on a topic, will enable them to gain ideas, see others' opinions, and feel part of the community. Seek input from students and engage all students. This type of environment not only strengthens science knowledge but also creates a sense of community within the classroom.

Using New Literacies Wisely

Thanks to modern technology, there are many other types of text that we can use with our students. Many of us incorporate blogs, articles found on websites, virtual field trips, and even videos into our classrooms as inexpensive forms of text. These types of text are often referred to as "new literacies," and they can play an important role in our science classrooms. Our students are growing up with technology, so digital texts serve as a way to connect the technology they use outside the classroom with their in-school learning. Therefore, there is a strong motivational aspect to new literacies.

While our students are bombarded with digital text, that doesn't mean that they are intelligent consumers of nonprint media. It is essential that students learn to view and interpret these texts. With the knowledge explosion occurring through new literacies, we have an even more important role to evaluate these new texts, and to help students evaluate any text they encounter.

Evaluating Digital Texts

Scientific digital texts should possess many of the same characteristics as quality trade books. To begin with, we expect the scientific information to be accurate and timely. We also want the text to be well written, appealing to our students, and include precise scientific vocabulary. Those are characteristics that we seek in diverse scientific texts.

However, there are additional important considerations we must think about as we evaluate digital texts that we don't typically think about as we examine scientific trade books. These unique considerations are important to bring to our students' attention because we need to teach students to intelligently evaluate digital texts. This will not only help our students to determine if the scientific texts they engage with in the classroom are of high quality but also make our students more effective consumers of digital text outside of our classrooms.

THE POWER OF A TWO-MINUTE ROOM SCAN

Take a quick look around your room. It might even be helpful to take a quick photo of all parts of your room. What types of local science text are displayed in the classroom? How are students engaging with it? If students haven't interacted with the posted material, is there a way that the text can be tied to the current learning, or does it need to be replaced?

What other types of local science text could be added to the classroom? If it is difficult to come up with new ideas for local text, look at other teachers' classrooms and brainstorm together types of local text that might be included. ✱

What makes digital text unique? Most of the differences pertain to two important qualities, *text creation* and *information access.*

Text Creation

Scientific trade books go through an extensive process to get from the original author's idea to printed form. Often the author's original concept for the text has to be approved by a group of people at a publishing company, and even after it is accepted, the actual manuscript is revised numerous times through the editorial process. Many different people at the publishing house will give feedback on the text. An idea does not typically move from an author's original idea to a printed trade book quickly.

On the other hand, a digital text can be quickly created and modified with only the author seeing the information. Anyone can post an idea on the Internet rather quickly as a blog entry, a YouTube video, or a presentation, without anyone else approving or even reviewing it. The fact that digital texts aren't subject to the same rigorous review and production process means that we must analyze digital texts even more closely than trade books. It's important to look at the address for the digital text. Where is this digital text on the Internet? Are the last three letters *.com, .org,* or *.net*? Almost anyone can post texts on such sites if he or she pays. We also have to look carefully at *.edu* addresses because students can create those digital texts (if the school has a site), but a researcher can also create a digital text with that domain name. This is why author information is so important with digital texts. As we try to better understand the creation of the text, we also have to think about how we access the digital text.

Information Access

Information access in digital text is very different than in trade books. With digital texts, we don't just turn pages, but instead we rely on various links to get additional information and view interactive images. If we have trouble finding our way around the website after opening additional links, can't get back to where we were before we clicked on links, or find that the links load very slowly, we may not want to use the digital text. There is also the concern that the digital text may not work with various browsers or on different devices.

Special Considerations for Digital Texts

The Digital Science Text Evaluation Guide in Figure 2.8 (also available in Appendix C) can help you determine the quality of scientific digital texts. While there are some areas on this guide that are similar to the Science Trade Book Evaluation Guide (see Figure 2.4), let's take a closer look at additional considerations we must think about with digital texts.

» **Science Content:** Since minimal steps and time can move an original idea to a published digital text, we have to pay special attention to the author's information. Often on digital texts there is an "About" section or a section titled "FAQ" (or "Frequently Asked Questions"), which may provide more information on the author. That is important because we want to ensure that the author of the digital text has the education or life experiences necessary to write the text. The author's name and background should be readily available to the reader.

» **Images:** Along with the standard illustrations and photographs often found in trade books, digital texts often contain interactive images. These interactive images, as well as any others that the author includes, should serve a purpose within the text. We also don't want to find ourselves distracted by any sound effects or movement of the images. The interactive images should be there to further our understanding of the scientific information.

APPENDIX C   Digital Science Text Evaluation Guide

AREA OF FOCUS	NOTES

Science Content
- ❍ Is there any background information about the author?
- ❍ Is there any misleading information?
- ❍ Are the information and copyright current?
- ❍ Is it free of stereotypes?
- ❍ Does the information extend beyond the text?

Images
- ❍ Are the illustrations realistic?
- ❍ Do the photographs support the text, and are they accompanied by credits?
- ❍ Are the drawings accurate in scale?
- ❍ Are there interactive visuals?

Writing
- ❍ Is it engaging for students?
- ❍ Is there a logical presentation?
- ❍ Does it include precise scientific terminology?
- ❍ Are the grammar and spelling correct?

Overall Design
- ❍ Are the layout and format appropriate?
- ❍ Is it appealing to students?

Text Access
- ❍ Is it easy to use?
- ❍ Does it work with various browsers?

◀ FIGURE 2.8

» **Writing:** Along with the customary areas to analyze, we want to make sure that grammar and spelling are correct. If the text contains many typographical or language errors, then more than likely nobody has reviewed the text except the author. It also makes you question the quality of the information within the text.

» **Overall Design:** Just as with trade books, we must look at how information is presented with digital text. Is it appealing and appropriate for the audience?

» **Text Access:** This area is unique to digital texts. We need to see how easy it is to access the digital text. We don't want to have to click multiple times to get to information. Likewise, does the text download quickly? All of the links in a digital text should work and help extend the information in the text. In addition, we have to be sure that diverse browsers can open the text so that all of our students will be able to view the text.

Digital text plays a key role in science classrooms, so it is important that we not only evaluate the texts but also teach our students to evaluate them. I'll discuss this more in Chapter 4.

Before Moving On

Our textbook should be only one of the many forms of text our students encounter in the science classroom. Science activities and experiments can be supplemented with trade books, e-books, local text, websites, and many other texts. As we focus on our students and our lesson's purpose, we can select a variety of texts that achieve our goals. Of course, having great texts available is only the beginning. It is similar to having boxes of fantastic science kits in our classroom closets. We have to teach students to access the information in those texts. Vocabulary plays a key role in that process. If students don't understand the terms they encounter, we can't expect them to gain content knowledge. Let's take a look at the suggestions in Chapter 3 for teaching our students to unlock the vocabulary terms in science texts.

3

Building Scientific Vocabulary Knowledge

To get our students thinking like scientists, we need to think about how we can best strengthen their scientific vocabulary. Think for just one minute about all of the terms we introduce students to in science. For example, we know that an introductory biology textbook contains approximately 3,500 new terms (Armstrong and Collier 1990)! While even our successful readers will need to have strategies in place to deal with those vocabulary demands, imagine the confusion our struggling readers and ELLs must experience when they try to comprehend a science textbook. If that number of new terms isn't mind-boggling enough, we have to realize that the science textbook is only one source of new terms in our classroom. As our students participate in hands-on science experiments and research online and in trade books, they encounter even more unfamiliar science terms.

THINK ABOUT **Vocabulary Strategies**

· ·

How do you typically teach and reinforce new terms students encounter in science? Are these strategies successful, and what concerns do you have with them?

How can we help our students to develop the vocabulary knowledge they need to understand scientific content? Well, it would be great if our students could just *pick up* new words through exposure to the scientific terms during experiments. That would be wonderful and make developing scientific vocabulary much easier, but unfortunately, research shows that this doesn't work. Our students need direct instruction in order to develop scientific vocabulary so that science content is accessible. This means that we must draw our students' attention to the terms we believe need to be taught in a systematic manner (Marzano and Pickering 2005).

Types of Terms Students Encounter

Before we begin thinking about how to teach different scientific terms, let's see what types of terms we want students to learn. Given the limited time we have in the science classroom, we have to be strategic as we determine which terms to teach. We can separate the terms students encounter in science texts into three tiers (Beck and McKeown 1985). Tier One words are those that students encounter on an everyday basis and that are already part of their oral vocabulary. Words such as *eat*, *small*, and *pet* are examples of Tier One words. While our students might see these words in science, these Tier One words are not words that we want to focus on for vocabulary instruction in science. Most of our students will already know these terms, and our ELL students will pick them up through their everyday use of the English language.

Then we have Tier Two terms. Unlike Tier One words, Tier Two terms aren't really part of our students' everyday vocabulary, but they are terms that students will encounter in various content areas, including science. For example, our students will see words like *noteworthy*, *replicate*, and *evaluate* in science, but chances are that they will also encounter these terms in social studies texts. However, Tier Two words aren't terms students encounter on a regular basis outside of content learning. Therefore, Tier Two terms need to be taught. For example, even if students can name the internal and external anatomy of a frog, if they can't understand what it means to *replicate* the experiment or to look for *noteworthy* results from their dissection, they will have difficulty strengthening their scientific knowledge. Therefore, it is important that students learn Tier Two terms.

Since students will encounter Tier Two terms in other content areas, it can be beneficial to spend time meeting with other teachers at the same grade level to discuss which terms are important for developing understanding in their content areas. Begin by looking at the science content you teach and determining which Tier Two terms you feel are integral to student understanding. These may be words that students encounter in their texts or use in class discussions. Focus on ones that students will see or hear repeatedly and are important to understanding the scientific concepts they are learning. Then sit down with other content area teachers, including the English language arts teacher, to determine if there are plans to teach or reinforce those Tier Two terms in their content areas. Other content area teachers may also have some Tier Two terms that you can reinforce in science.

It is important to note that Tier Two terms also include multi-meaning words. Multi-meaning words can be especially problematic for our students because while students may see them in other content areas or know of a familiar, everyday meaning for the terms, they may not know the terms' scientific meanings. For example, our students may use *table* and *fault* in everyday conversations, but they may not be familiar with the scientific definition of those terms. ELLs can especially experience confusion when they encounter multi-meaning words and are unaware that the terms have more than one meaning.

Finally, there are Tier Three terms. Unlike Tier Two terms, Tier Three terms are typically seen only in a specific content area, such as science. It is impossible to understand scientific content without a knowledge of these terms, and yet our students will often not encounter the Tier Three terms unless they are reading scientific texts or participating in a science class. For example, we know that science terms such as *metamorphosis* and *asteroid* are not part of our students' everyday speaking vocabulary. Therefore, we will need to be sure to provide a great deal of reinforcement for these terms in our science classrooms. Seeing or hearing a Tier Three term one or two times is not enough for students to remember it. This is important to keep in mind as we plan our science instruction.

Figure 3.1 contains examples of Tier Two and Tier Three science terms. Instead of listing multi-meaning words under the Tier Two column, I chose to put them in a separate column, since they can be especially confusing for students.

Now that you are aware of the terms you need to teach, you can think about the best way to teach those words in your classroom.

Principles for Vocabulary Instruction

There are four key principles that can help guide vocabulary instruction:

» Think smaller than the word level.
» Understand word relationships.

SAMPLE SCIENCE TERMS BY CATEGORY

Multi-meaning Words	Tier Two Words	Tier Three Words
agitate	adapt	abiotic factor
cell	analyze	anemometer
culture	classify	bacteria
draw	collaborate	carcinogen
fault	conduct	DNA
material	diminish	isotope
plates	essential	lithosphere
property	infer	molecule
race	investigate	photosynthesis
table	observe	species
volume	predict	velocity

◀ FIGURE 3.1

» Maintain students' scientific interest.

» Encourage wide reading.

As we use these four vocabulary principles to guide our science instruction, we can ensure that we are connecting literacy and science in a meaningful way that will benefit and strengthen our students' science vocabulary. I'm sure none of us wants to go back to the days of providing students with a list of science terms prior to the exploration of a science topic and then having them memorize the terms and their definitions so they can regurgitate them at a specific time on a test. Chances are many of us remember a similar experience and are still trying to forget it. How many terms did we learn this way and remember long enough to help us with understanding science content? Asking students to memorize words in this way will result in a very superficial understanding of scientific concepts and may even encourage our students to falsely believe that science is just a list of facts to memorize (Songer and Linn 1991). We all know that scientific understanding is much more than that, so let's look

TAKE ACTION

CATEGORIZING VOCABULARY TERMS

Copy the Key Science Terms Chart in Appendix D and look over the next topic you will teach in science. Think about the science experiments the students will be conducting in class and the texts they may be using, and determine which Tier Two (including multi-meaning) and Tier Three terms you believe will play a key role in students' ability to understand the science content. Choose terms that students will need to know to understand key scientific concepts and that students will probably encounter multiple times during a unit of study. List the terms on the Key Science Terms Chart. If possible, discuss and complete the chart with a group of other teachers at your grade level who may be working with your students in other content areas. That way it will be possible to determine if multi-meaning terms or other Tier Two terms can be reinforced with students through other content area lessons. After the chart is complete, keep a copy of it handy so that you can refer to the chart as you read the rest of this chapter, and think about which strategies you might use for the scientific terms you plan to teach. ✳

at the four principles and how they might guide vocabulary instruction in our science classroom.

Thinking Smaller than the Word Level

Often when we think about vocabulary, we think about words, whole words. However, not all scientific terms are best taught as whole word units. In fact, while we might feel that the word *vocabulary* automatically refers to *words* that we want students to learn, it is important that we realize that we don't always have to teach entire words to strengthen our students' vocabulary. We can actually help students more at times by teaching meaningful units within words because they can use these word parts to recognize new science words they encounter.

Studying Morphemes

When we look at the terms we plan to teach, it is obvious that many of the words are composed of smaller units of meaning, called morphemes. Look at the list of terms on the Key Science Terms Chart you created earlier in the chapter. Are there units of meaning such as *-osis*, *hydro-*, *-meter*, *bio-*, or *-ology* in some of the terms your students are learning? Each of these meaningful parts (or morphemes) has meaning. For example, *hydro-* (*hydr-*) refers to water or fluid. Therefore, by knowing the meaning of that morpheme, students will more easily be able to recognize and ultimately understand terms such as *hydrocephalus*, *hydrogen*, *hydrodynamics*, and *hydroelectric*.

Morphemes also include prefixes and suffixes that are common in many words. Often these morphemes are referred to as bound morphemes because they have meaning only when attached to another morpheme. While *-s* has no meaning when written by itself, it does have meaning when it is part of a larger word, such as *invertebrates*. The *-s* indicates more than one. Similarly, the prefix *re-* is a morpheme because the letters mean *to do again* or *repeat* when *re-* is at the beginning of some units of meaning. Our students will encounter many of the morphemes shown in Figure 3.2. This chart (Padak et al. 2008) is a valuable tool for morphemic analysis.

USEFUL MORPHEMES

Prefixes	
a-, ab-, abs-	away, from
auto-	self
di-, dif-, dis-	apart, in different directions, not
inter-	between, among
per-	through, thorough
post-	after
pro-	forward, ahead
tele-	from afar
tra-, tran-, trans-	across, change

Assimilating Prefixes	
ad-	to, toward, add to
con-, com-, col-	with, together
in-, im-, il-	in, on, into (directional); not (negative)
ob-	up against, in the way

Parallel Latin and Greek Prefixes (Latin/Greek)	
contra-, contro-, counter- / *anti-*	against
circu-, circum- / *peri-*	around
multi- / *poly-*	many
super-, sur- / *hyper-*	over
sub- / *hypo-*	under, below

Bases	
cred-, credit-	believe
cur-, curs-, cours-	run, go
dict-	say, tell, speak

◀ FIGURE 3.2

Bases *(continued)*

duc-, duct-	lead
fac-, fic-, fact-, fect-	do, make
mis-, mit-	to send
pon-, pos-, posit-	put, place
scrib-, script-	write
sent-, sens-	think, feel
solv-, solut-	free, loosen
tend-, tens-, tenu-	stretch, thin
terr-	earth
trac-, tract-	pull, draw, drag
ven-, vent-	come
volu-, volute-, volv-	roll

Parallel Latin and Greek Bases (Latin/Greek)

am(a)-, amat- / philo-	love
aqua- / hydro-	water
fort-, forc- / dynamo-	power, strong
lumen-, luc- / photo-	light
nat-, natur- / gen-, gener-	be born, give birth, produce
nov- / neo-	new
omni- / pant-	all, every
ped- / pod-	foot, feet
spec-, spect- / scop-	look at, watch
viv-, vit- / bio-	live, life
voc-, vok- / phon-	voice, call

◀ FIGURE 3.2 *(continued)*

Suffixes	
-ance, -ancy, -ence, -ency	state or quality
-ant, -ent	in the process, having the characteristics of
-arium, -orium	place for, container for
-ate	do
-ation	state or condition
-crat	ruler
-cracy	one who believes in rule by
-ify	to make
-ologist	one who studies
-ology	study of
-or, -er	one who does
-ose, -ous, -eous, -ious	full of
-phobe	one who fears
-phobia	fear

◀ **FIGURE** 3.2 *(continued)*

As we already know, we can't teach all unfamiliar science terms, but by helping our students, including ELLs and struggling readers, develop an understanding of morphemes, we are preparing them to be able to independently learn future unfamiliar terms they may encounter in science (Vacca and Vacca 2002). Developing their morphemic knowledge will exponentially expand the number of words they can read.

Introducing the Idea of Morphemes

There are a couple of different ways that we can introduce the concept of morpheme in the science classroom that will catch students' interest. One way is to ask students if they know the longest word in the English language. What student doesn't love cool and unique facts? Chances are they will not know the word *pneumonoultramicroscopicsilicovolcanoconiosis*, and it is a fun way to introduce the idea of morphemes. Explain to students that there are actually eight smaller units of meaning (morphemes) that make up the word (*pneumono, ultra, micro, scopic, silico, volcano, coni, osis*). By figuring out these morphemes, we not only learn the meaning of this word but also learn information we can use to understand the meaning of other scientific terms we encounter.

Students may even already be familiar with some of the units of meaning we find in this term. Ask the class if any part of the term *pneumonoultramicroscopicsilicovolcanoconiosis* looks familiar. Chances are students might recognize *volcano* or perhaps *micro*. Do they have any idea what the familiar morphemes mean in the word? Can they explain their guesses? Where else have they seen these word parts? After circling familiar morphemes, ask students again if they see any other word parts that may look familiar. Students, depending on their grade level, may mention *scopic, pneumono,* and *osis*. Ask students to brainstorm other words they know that contain these morphemes. Again, some students might predict the meaning for some of the morphemes, but the class can research online to determine if that meaning is correct. Then have students work in groups to research the meaning of any remaining word parts in the term *pneumonoultramicroscopicsilicovolcanoconiosis* to see if they can determine a definition for the term. The actual definition is "a lung disease caused by the inhalation of fine silicone dust particles." Students will be able to determine a meaning that is very similar to the dictionary one through their morphemic analysis of the term.

Another idea is to use students' interest in technology to introduce the concept of morphemes. Ask students to brainstorm a list of technology terms that are the result of putting smaller units of meaning together (e.g., *Internet, smartphone, website, Photoshop, PowerPoint, email, Facebook*). Ask students the meaning of individual morphemes in each word and discuss how the morphemes create the new word. Explain that knowing morphemes will enable them to analyze many words found in science lessons.

Using Morphemic Analysis to Expand Science Vocabulary: Sniglets

I always tell preservice and inservice teachers that anytime we can combine laughter and education, we have a good thing because teachers have to have a sense of humor. We can actually thank a comedian, Rich Hall, for the idea for a great activity we can use to focus our students' attention on morphemes in scientific words. Hall uses the term *sniglet* to refer to any word that isn't in the dictionary but should be. Therefore, I like to have students create sniglets with morphemes they frequently see in science (Altieri 2011).

For this activity, I select some morphemes I want students to learn, including affixes, such as prefixes and suffixes. Figure 3.2 is a great list to consider. Then students work with partners to create a sniglet by combining three to five of the morphemes. The meaning of the sniglet students create is a combination of the meanings of the morphemes. I limit students to using five morphemes because I find creating a sniglet with more than five morphemes usually results in students remembering very few of the morphemes they use. (While a couple of students might want to string together a lot of morphemes to make the longest possible sniglet, often they can't even say the sniglet they create if it contains a large number of morphemes.) After students select the three to five morphemes, they write their sniglet on a sheet of paper, write the definition for the term, use the term in a sentence, and draw a visual. Students might even enjoy seeing if others can figure out the definition of their sniglet prior to seeing the written definition. These sniglet pages can be put together to create a class book, e-book, or PowerPoint presentation.

Figure 3.3 shows three examples of student sniglets. The student examples contain a wide variety of morphemes we often see in science, such as *auto-*, *hydro-*, and *bio-*, along with suffixes, such as *-ology* and *-ation*. All of these are morphemes that the students will encounter again in science. By thinking about the meaning of the morphemes, creating the sniglet, writing the definition, using the sniglet in a sentence, and drawing a visual to explain it, the students will be much more likely to be able to decode future science terms they encounter with these morphemes.

If you want to reinforce the learning of morphemes or provide additional practice on morphemic analysis with a small group of struggling students, you can write individual morphemes on the sides of five or six paper cubes. Then a student can roll the cubes. Each student then selects three of the morphemes to create a sniglet and writes the sniglet and its definition on a small piece of paper. Then each student takes a turn orally sharing with the other students the definition of his or her sniglet and sees if the other students can figure out the

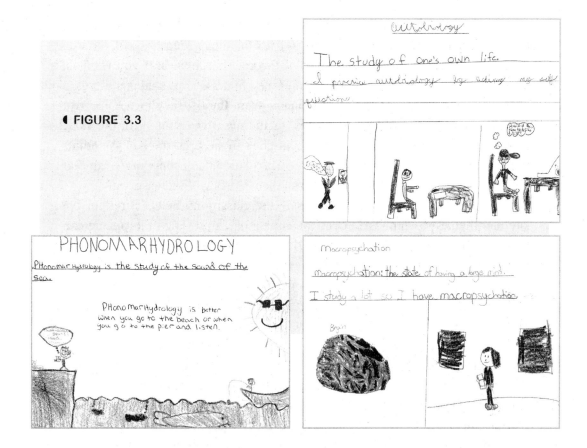

◖ FIGURE 3.3

morphemes used. If necessary, students can refer to a list of the morphemes that are written on the cubes and their definitions while completing this activity.

Practicing and Reinforcing Morphemic Knowledge: Word Dissection

Just as students dissect in a science lab, they can also dissect words they encounter in the science classroom using their knowledge of morphemes. This gives them a chance to directly apply the process of analyzing morphemes to the science they are engaging with in class. Look through a chunk of text students will be reading in their next science class. This text may be a website, the written steps to a science experiment, or even a textbook. Determine eight to ten morphemes that you believe are valuable for students to learn. These should be morphemes seen multiple times in the text. Have students list those morphemes in a column on the left side of a sheet of paper. Then allow students to work individually or collaboratively in pairs or small groups to skim through a chunk of text, looking for examples of the key morphemes. If you want to, let students earn points for the morphemes they find. Perhaps students can earn five points for every key science morpheme from the list they locate and two additional points for other morphemes, including affixes, found in the same words. Students can compete against themselves by keeping track of the points they earn at various times during the year. As students become more familiar with dissecting words to find morphemes, their scores will increase.

We can extend this activity outside the classroom. Select three to five key morphemes to emphasize over the course of a unit. Each morpheme can be written on a sheet of chart paper. Then have students note whenever they hear or see one of the key morphemes in a word outside of school (e.g., a family conversation, movie, song, commercial). See how many different terms students find that contain the morpheme over the course of the science unit. This not only reinforces morphemic knowledge but encourages the connection of classroom science learning with the learning that occurs outside the formal educational setting.

Not all words will lend themselves well to morphemic analysis. Other terms may best be taught by focusing student attention on the entire word. However, whether we decide to teach science terms through morphemic analysis or drawing students' attention to the entire term, we need to focus student attention on the relationships between scientific concepts we want students to understand.

Understanding Word Relationships

As students develop their scientific vocabulary knowledge, it is important that they realize how scientific terms relate to other terms so that they have a deeper understanding of the content.

In order to truly understand scientific words, our students need opportunities to focus on the use of terms they already know in relationship to other words they encounter (Blachowicz et al. 2006). The idea of thematically linking words is not new to the educational field, but research continues to show that this linking is very important in order for our students to develop an understanding of new terms and science content. In fact, research with middle school students who have learning disabilities shows that students who associate new terms to other words learn a great deal more vocabulary than those who are taught via the dictionary method (Bos et al. 2001). There are many ways we can help students to associate new terms with other words.

Focusing on Word Relationships: Prereading Brainstorm

One way to begin focusing on word relationships is through asking students to brainstorm information about scientific words. To start, select four or five key scientific terms the students will encounter in a chunk of text. Then put each of these terms on a large sheet of chart paper. For example, if students will be studying the concept of *motion*, they may encounter terms such as *air resistance*, *friction*, *force*, and *kinetic energy*. Give each group of students one of the sheets of chart paper. Ask students to brainstorm what they already know about the key term on their paper. Then ask students to skim through the text selection until they find their vocabulary term. They can note sentences or headings that contain the term and list ideas for the term's meaning. Do they see the mention of any other scientific terms with the keyword? Perhaps the word *load* is seen in the discussion about *force*. If so, the group of students investigating *force* can write the term *load* on their chart as a word that relates to *force*. Also, ask students if there are any other terms in the reading that relate to the key term. This might include synonyms or antonyms. Have students add those words to the sheet. Then have the students orally share what they put on their chart papers. As part of this discussion, talk about how the written words or terms relate to the key terms. Display these chart papers in the classroom throughout the science unit as local text (see the discussion of local text in Chapter 2). When students encounter one of the key terms in the unit, draw their attention back to the charts. Students may even decide that there are other words they want to add to the charts as the unit progresses. The goal is simply to get students thinking about relationships among scientific concepts.

Building Relationships: Science Term Scavenger Hunt

Another idea that can get students thinking about relationships among scientific concepts they will be learning is to have a science term scavenger hunt (Vaugh, Crawley, and Mountain 1979). This activity is a good way to introduce a topic of study, pique students' curiosity, and encourage them to look at the relationships between science terms. Begin by giving small groups of students a list of unfamiliar science terms that relate to their next unit of study. Read through the list of terms with the class so that all students have at least heard the terms. Then explain that each group of students is going to go on a scavenger hunt to determine the meaning of each term and then either find or create an example of it (e.g., a diagram, a video clip, a description in a trade book, a model, an infographic, or even an actual example). Each group of students decides which student will find an example of each term on the list. The student responsible for finding each example puts his or her initials next to the term. Since each student will be finding examples of multiple terms, allow students a week to locate or make their examples. While the terms may be new to your students, that doesn't mean that they can't research and determine the meaning either by talking with adults or looking at digital or traditional texts. Encourage students to be creative and if possible to draw or create an example rather than photocopy one out of a text. This will also help students remember the term.

For example, the following is a list of scientific terms appropriate for a class beginning a study of the major organ systems:

esophagus	mandible	small intestines	lungs
patella	trachea	salivary glands	phalanges
diaphragm	liver	clavicle	alveoli

On the day students bring their examples to class, give each small group a sheet of paper with three columns. Each column should have a category at the top of it. For the terms above, these categories might be *skeletal system*, *digestive system*, and *respiratory system*. After providing a very brief class overview on each system, have students work in their small groups to share the examples they brought in and any information they know about their examples from finding them. Then the students in each group determine which of the major organ systems each example belongs in and list the term in the appropriate column. Check out Figure 3.4 to see how a group sheet will look. Through a class discussion, students can share their sheets and discuss any interesting information they were able to learn about their terms. If students create examples for terms, these examples can be put on display in the classroom.

Skeletal	Respiratory	Digestive
mandible	trachea	small intestines
patella	alveoli	esophagus
phalanges	lungs	liver
clavicle	diaphragm	salivary glands

◀ FIGURE 3.4

Reinforcing Word Relationships: Semantic Feature Analysis

Obviously we can't just focus on word relationships prior to learning content. Students need to see, hear, and read the science terms many times in order to truly learn them. The only way to do that is to continue reinforcing word relationships throughout a scientific unit of study.

A semantic feature analysis (Anders and Boss 1986), which helps students to understand the attributes of key scientific concepts, can be a great strategy to use and add to during a unit of study. After students learn information on a scientific concept through hands-on activities and exposure to text, help them to think about the information they know and how the scientific concepts relate. Begin by listing the key concepts you want students to compare and contrast down the left side of a piece of paper. Then list the attributes or features of these concepts that students will be comparing across the top of the page, creating a chart or matrix. As students think about each key concept, they put a + or a 0 in each column, denoting whether that concept has that attribute (+) or does not possess that attribute (0), or a question mark if they are not sure. Upon the completion of the semantic feature analysis, students can compare and contrast the concepts based on the attributes, developing a better understanding of their similarities and differences and the relationships between terms. Figure 3.5 shows a semantic feature analysis on living organisms.

As we look at a semantic feature analysis, such as the one in Figure 3.5, we can ask students questions regarding it. Basic questions such as, "Which living organisms are predators?" are useful, but questions such as, "Which two organisms have the least in common?" promote higher-level thinking. They require students to synthesize information they see on the matrix. Students can also

SEMANTIC FEATURE ANALYSIS ON LIVING ORGANISMS

	Predator	Cold-Blooded	Herbivore	Egg-Producing	Produces Milk for Young
Lizard	+	+	0	+	0
Horse	0	0	+	0	+
Snake	+	+	0	+	0
Lion	+	0	0	0	+
Mouse	0	0	+	0	+

◀ FIGURE 3.5

create their own questions for other students to answer about the chart. While the creation of the semantic feature analysis is important, the discussion that follows can be particularly beneficial for reinforcing ideas about relationships.

A semantic feature analysis can also serve as an excellent strategy to compare topics studied over the course of a year. For example, students can compare the characteristics of different animals' *digestive, reproductive, circulatory,* and *respiratory* systems. Not only will this reinforce the terms and attributes, but it will help students to identify the similarities and differences between these systems in different animals.

Of course nothing is black-and-white. Some scientific concepts may *always, sometimes,* or *rarely* possess a given attribute. In that case, you might have students put a number between 1 and 5 in each column for rarely (1), sometimes (3), or usually (5), or perhaps to indicate a range, such as very few (1) to very many (5) of the members of a group possess an attribute. One example might be looking at four or five viruses. Two of the attributes might be *affects infants and children* and *affects adults.* If one of the viruses under discussion is the Enterovirus 68, students will learn that it primarily infects infants and children, but in approximately 25 percent of the cases prior to 2005, it infected adults (Phillip 2014). Therefore, they might wonder what to put in the two attribute columns. While you can't say the virus affects *only* children, it affects that population more than others. Students might consider putting a 4 in the "Affects Infants and Children" column and a 1 under the "Affects Adults" column next to Enterovirus 68.

Reinforcing and Assessing: List-Group-Label

After students complete a unit of study, there are additional ways to reinforce word relationships. These suggestions also serve as ways to informally assess what students know about scientific concepts and expand that knowledge.

List-group-label (Taba 1967) is a great strategy to use with almost any scientific topic. Begin by asking students to brainstorm approximately twenty-five words that relate to a scientific topic. As students state terms, list each one on a whiteboard. Figure 3.6 is an example of what such a list might look like if students used the activity after a unit on extreme weather.

As you list each of the terms, repeat it. If a term is unfamiliar to a student, it will now at least be in that student's listening vocabulary. Depending on the level and needs of the class, you may choose to have the students read the complete list aloud or ask if there are any terms on it that they do not recognize. Then have students work in small groups to create categories of words. Any three to five words can create a category as long as students put a title for the group that states the relationship between the terms. Students can also use the listed terms in more than one category. In the example given, a group of students might decide to create a category with the terms *weather maps*, *Richter scale*, *thermometer*, and *weather satellites* and title the category *Ways*

EXTREME WEATHER TERMS

atmosphere	hydrosphere	lithosphere	surface
radiation	convection	expansion	contraction
light energy	heat energy	water cycle	cold front
precipitation	barometric pressure	humidity	wind
temperature	weather satellites	hurricanes	tornadoes
blizzards	drought	avalanche	thermometer
weather maps	Richter scale		

◀ FIGURE 3.6

to Measure Weather. If students create a category with more than five terms, encourage them to talk within their group about the terms in that category to see if they can determine a way to split the category into two groups. This encourages students to think more specifically about each term and its meaning. The group discussion is invaluable. By talking about the terms and relationships, students are helping each other to develop their scientific knowledge. Some students may have additional insight to share about some of the terms from readings or discussions during the unit that other students may not have experienced. Also, others may have difficulty remembering specific scientific terms and students can scaffold their peers' learning through discussion.

If students finish creating categories but still struggle to place a term or two in a category, encourage them to consider modifying one of their category titles to include the extra terms. That will mean thinking about the relationship of the terms and perhaps broadening a category slightly. After the students finish the activity, ask each group of students to share with the rest of the class some of their categories.

Reinforcing: Categorization Cards

Another activity that can reinforce relationships between science terms is to create categorization cards, which students can sort into categories. As you introduce students to key scientific terms during a unit, create a card for each term. After the creation of approximately twenty cards, there will be enough cards for students to categorize. Along with writing the scientific term and a definition on each card, consider putting a meaningful visual that reinforces the term's meaning for students. This visual might be a photograph or even clip art. Using visuals on the cards will help all students remember the terms but is especially helpful to ELLs and struggling readers.

Another possibility is to provide the list of scientific terms and have students create a set of individual cards outside of class. Students can use these cards for a variety of identification and categorization activities. Perhaps students can sort categorization cards of animals into groups of herbivores and omnivores, or maybe you want to have students categorize cards with plant names into groups that grow in similar habitats. Also, you can use this activity to focus student attention on morphemes by having students sort scientific terms into groups that have a morpheme in common. Categories can even be student-driven. Allow students to sort the cards into categories and see if others can figure out the categories based on the science terms they group together. In order to create the categories, students will be thinking about the terms, their meanings, and their relationships.

Creating and Maintaining Scientific Interest

Not only must we focus our students' attention on scientific terms that we believe they need to learn and the relationships among them, but we need to strongly encourage our students' intrinsic interest in the scientific words they encounter. This is especially important because we can't teach every new word our students will encounter in scientific text, and if our students develop an intrinsic interest in science terminology (or words in general), they can quickly expand their scientific vocabulary because they will want to seek out the meaning to new words. Think about how much we learn when we have intrinsic motivation. Our goal is to get our students to have that level of interest in scientific words and to find them unique and intriguing.

Many adults who love reading have an interest in and awareness of words. Do you ever find yourself repeating a new word you heard someone say or saw in a text because you like the way it rolls off your tongue or looks in print? We can also see this interest, or word consciousness (Graves and Watts-Taffe 2002), with very young children. They constantly play with words just because they have a natural curiosity about them. Do you remember that feeling? I see the interest and enjoyment elementary students get from Dr. Seuss books, tongue twisters, and joke books. The important question is how we can maintain this word consciousness, or interest in words, with our older students.

We know that *choice* can be an important element in all teaching. Choice is powerful because students feel like they have input. I believe that choice can play a key role in maintaining and strengthening our students' intrinsic interest. By allowing our students choice, or the opportunity to select some of the science terms they will learn, we can motivate them to learn the terms. Often we may have specific terms we believe students should learn, and we may worry that if we provide choice, students won't learn those specific terms. However, allowing choice doesn't mean that we have no input on the selection of terms taught. Each of the activities I describe in this section fosters word consciousness and also allows our students an element of choice as they learn scientific phrases and words.

Figurative Language: Playing with Words Science-Style

To begin with, let's show our students how much fun it is just to play with words and, more specifically, science terms. In my opinion, the best way to do that is to get our students playing with words science-style. There are numerous examples where a phrase we use in everyday language makes use of scientific terms but has a different meaning than its literal definition. Phrases such as *I got my wires crossed, out of steam, firing on all cylinders,* and *blow a fuse* are a few examples. If a phrase is unfamiliar, we can ask students to research the phrase's origin. For example, what is the literal meaning of *I got my wires crossed*? What occurs when that happens in science? How do they think that literal meaning might relate to the figurative meaning of the phrase? Students will also enjoy finding other examples of figurative phrases that relate to scientific concepts through online research and talking with adults.

Science Term of the Week

Another idea is to have a science term of the week. We all encounter words that just stand out to us. Perhaps we love the spelling or the way the term looks in a particular sentence. However, the science term of the week can be any term that ties to science that we think others will enjoy learning. Initially, you may want to select the science term of the week, but as the year progresses, encourage students to bring in fascinating science terms they see and want to learn. Our students can find these terms in advertisements they hear, billboards or articles they read, and YouTube videos they view. As part of this we can also share with our students websites, such as www.thesaurus.com and www.wordcentral.com, that are free and include synonyms and antonyms for a variety of words. Our goal is to interest our students in new words they encounter.

As students encounter new and interesting words they want to share, we can encourage them to research the history behind the science terms, because often words have interesting trivia surrounding them. We might also have our students create entries for a class or school blog (see the site www.tingoed

.com for one possible model) highlighting their words of the day. As part of this activity, students can incorporate videos and other multimedia presentations into their entries.

Personal Science Vocabulary Journals

We can also develop interest in science terms by having students keep personal science vocabulary journals. In these journals students will list interesting or unique scientific terms they encounter outside of the classroom that pertain to the science unit they are studying. Students might encounter the words in a text, hear them when talking with family members about the topic, or learn about them in some other way. As students encounter these terms, they can list them in their personal science vocabulary journals along with where they saw or heard them. Then at the end of the science unit, students can revisit these journals.

One idea is to have students get in small groups and share their lists of scientific terms from their personal science journals. Each group of students can then pick a favorite word from the ones their group members share and plan a creative way to teach the rest of the class the new science term. Students might create a visual, write a short rap, or act out the term. Each group can have a few minutes to share its creation at the end of the unit.

Important Word Rating

Taking vocabulary terms and assigning them a knowledge rating is not new and was encouraged as a vocabulary strategy in the 1980s (Blachowicz 1986). However, important word rating encourages students to be creative and look at diverse texts. It also incorporates ideas from two popular vocabulary strategies, the vocabulary self-collection strategy (Haggard 1986) and the strategy called "ten important words plus" (Yopp and Yopp 2003). For this activity, begin by dividing the class into groups of four or five students. Then ask each student to bring in a text that relates to a scientific topic they have been studying. Students might choose to bring in a website article, a picture book, song lyrics, or even a poem.

The day students bring the texts to class, have each group look through their materials to determine five scientific terms they think are important and relate to the science topic they are studying. Of course it won't take long for a student to ask, "What is an *important* word?" This question can spur a great class discussion as students debate the qualities that make a term important. Is an important word a word that is difficult to pronounce, a term shown in bold or italicized font, a word they see repeated numerous times in the text, or a really long word? There is not one right answer. However, thinking about and discussing the way in which words are drawn to our students' attention in text can serve as a valuable reflection activity. Have each group of students write their five important words on a sheet of paper. Then ask a group to tell you one of the terms they believe to be an important scientific term and why they feel the term is important. Did any of the other groups choose the same word, a form of the word, or a similar term? Compile a list of the scientific terms on chart paper or a sheet of paper using a document camera, and ask any other groups that have one of the shared terms on their list to draw a line through it or otherwise mark it so they don't repeat it when it's their turn to share. Repeat this with each group until all groups have the opportunity to share their terms.

Then give each student the two-page Group Knowledge Rating Sheet, shown in Figure 3.7. (A reproducible of this form is available in Appendix E.) If the class list contains more than ten words, point out that you are going to choose eight to ten of the words. Circle those eight to ten scientific terms on which you want to focus your students' attention, and ask all students to list the circled science terms down the left side of their two-page Knowledge Rating Sheet. Now tell the students that you want them to show their level of knowledge for each term. Of course they may not have seen some of the terms before, but chances are they may have encountered others during the unit or through reading completed outside the classroom.

Have each student circle the appropriate heading next to each term (i.e., circle either "Unfamiliar," "Know a Little," or "Know It Well") showing his or her level of knowledge for each scientific term. If students think that they know a little about the term, have them write what they know about the term in the provided area. Do they remember where they saw the term or have a general idea of its use? If students believe they know the term well, ask them to define it on the sheet. I also ask that they use this column only if they think they can explain the term to others in the class. That way they aren't just copying

APPENDIX E   **Group Knowledge Rating Sheet**

Science Term	1 pt.	3 pts.	5 pts.	Points
	Unfamiliar	Know a Little What do you know?	Know It Well / Can Teach It Write the definition.	

Science Term	1 pt.	3 pts.	5 pts.	Points
	Unfamiliar	Know a Little What do you know?	Know It Well / Can Teach It Write the definition.	

Science Term	1 pt.	3 pts.	5 pts.	Points
	Unfamiliar	Know a Little What do you know?	Know It Well / Can Teach It Write the definition.	

Science Term	1 pt.	3 pts.	5 pts.	Points
	Unfamiliar	Know a Little What do you know?	Know It Well / Can Teach It Write the definition.	

Science Term	1 pt.	3 pts.	5 pts.	Points
	Unfamiliar	Know a Little What do you know?	Know It Well / Can Teach It Write the definition.	

Individual student points _____

Group points _____

Class points _____

◀ FIGURE 3.7

a definition out of a text. By having them write the definition in their own words, I know if they can truly explain the concept or if there is confusion. Students put their points earned for each science term at the end of the line, under "Points." Then they add up their points from both pages to get a total to put on the line next to "Individual Student Points." Their goal is to increase this score through collaborating with others.

Explain to the students that they are now going to expand their vocabulary through working with their group members. Give each group a clean copy of both pages of the Group Knowledge Rating Sheet. Review the first scientific term as a class. Ask all of the students to look at their individually completed sheets and then as a group determine which students in the group were able to mark the highest level of knowledge about the term on their sheets. The goal is for the students with the highest level of knowledge in the group to teach others in the group the scientific term. Ask the student or students with the highest score for the first science term to teach the others in their group what they know about the term. One person can be the recorder, who writes the science terms down the left side of the paper and marks the group's score on the clean sheet as they talk about each term. Therefore, if one person in a group knows the term well, the only way the recorder can circle "Know It Well" for that term is if the student who knows the term teaches the other members of the group the meaning of the word and the recorder writes the definition on the group sheet. The students in each group work together to raise their group's score for each word and record the total score on the "Group Points" line. Using the Knowledge Rating Sheet with groups requires students to collaborate and learn from others' knowledge.

After the students finish rating their group knowledge, it is time to bring the students together as a class to discuss their charts. Ask groups that have a high level of knowledge on a scientific term to share their knowledge of the term with the rest of the class. While multiple groups may know it well, that doesn't mean that they will all have the exact same information to share about the concept. After whole-class discussion of a term, if other groups feel that they can rate their knowledge level higher for that term, have them mark their new level and change their score in the "Points" column for that term on the chart. After the whole-class discussion, each group can list their new score on the line next to "Class Points." While the points might motivate students, the purpose of this activity is for students to collaborate together after reading self-selected texts to increase their knowledge of scientific vocabulary.

Reinforcing Science Terms: Word Cloud

Let's think about interesting and motivating ways we can reinforce the science terms our students are learning in class. First of all, I love to have students create a word cloud. These clouds are visual representations of words and their relationships, and students at all grade levels enjoy creating them. There are several free sites our students can use on the Internet, including www.wordle .net, tagul.com, and www.tagxedo.com, to create their own clouds. If we ask students to brainstorm a list of science terms that relate to a science unit they are completing, this activity can serve as a great review and lead into a final class discussion. After the discussion, students can select scientific terms to put in their word clouds. However, we can also allow our students to type in their notes from a science writing assignment to create a word cloud. After students complete their word clouds, they can share them with other students.

One seventh-grade science teacher decided to have each of her students create a word cloud representing one of the systems of the body. The students could use any terms they could recognize and explain. For example, Figure 3.8 shows one student's word cloud representing the respiratory system.

While Figure 3.8 is an example created at www.wordle .net, this student was able to take the words she chose and create a word cloud in the shape of a lung at www.tagxedo.com. Another classmate chose to create a word cloud in the shape of a

◀ FIGURE 3.8

hand and included terms such as skeletal, joints, cartilage, tendons, and ligaments, while another student created a heart word cloud using terms such as pacemaker, plaque, valve, atria, and bicuspid. After the students created the word clouds, the teacher asked them to share their word clouds to see if other students could guess the systems represented. Then students worked with partners to see if they could identify each of the scientific terms in each other's clouds. The partners worked together with each other to develop a better understanding of the terms listed.

This activity doesn't have to occur at the end of a unit. Students can also create a word cloud at the beginning of a science unit to see how many terms they can think of that tie to a topic, and then they can create another word cloud after they finish a science unit. Not only will this provide an informal assessment of the vocabulary students are learning, but our students will be able to see their own scientific vocabulary growth during the unit.

Reinforcing and Reviewing: Science Dictionary and ABC Science Book

While picture dictionaries are popular with early elementary grades, I don't think we realize the potential of creating subject-specific dictionaries in the upper elementary and middle school grades. These dictionaries can be especially beneficial for and serve as a way to support struggling readers or ELLs. For the science dictionary, have students write, define, and illustrate terms they want to remember in a journal. Individual students develop their own dictionaries, so the number of science terms will vary. The definition in the dictionary might come from an online source, their text, or a class discussion. If students can use their science dictionaries for quizzes, it will motivate them to keep the dictionaries up-to-date with new technical terms they need extra reinforcement to remember.

We can also ask our students to create an ABC science book. This review of a science topic is a fun way to build and reinforce content vocabulary that pertains to a specific science topic. Begin this activity by allowing each student to select a letter of the alphabet from a bag. Then ask each student to take a minute to think of a science term that ties to the science topic and begins with the letter he or she is holding. If there are more letters of the alphabet than students, keep the remaining letters, and let the class as a whole decide on the term or phrase for each of those letters. Discourage the use of phrases beginning with *a* or *the* or *some* because the idea is to build scientific vocabulary. For example, if students are studying weather, we want to avoid having a student who selects the letter *a* use the phrase *a meteorologist* or *a hurricane* when there are scientific terms related to weather that begin with the letter *a*. Trying not to use those phrases challenges students as they think about the terms that relate to the topic. If a student can't come up with a term or phrase, let that student call on a few other students to provide ideas, and then the student can determine the one to use. Discuss each of the terms and phrases as you add them to a class list on the topic.

In Figure 3.9, you can see an example of how one teacher used this activity with students who were studying animal adaptations. Here you can see one group's example was an X-ray fish for the letter *X*. In this instance, students worked together in groups of six, and each group of students used three or four letters of the alphabet. The student groups made a page for each letter they were given. This page included the term that began with the letter, a visual, and an explanation of the concept. From the example in Figure 3.9, we can see the students' knowledge of the concept of structural adaptation through the information they wrote on their page.

After students share the pages with the class, you can put them together into a book to share with or give to a younger grade level. Along with reinforcing students' vocabulary, this activity can be one way to introduce future topics of scientific study to younger students.

Reinforcing and Remembering: Keyword Method

Research supports the use of images as mnemonic devices (Carney and Levin 2002) to help us remember information. Like many of us, our students grow up learning phrases such as *King Phillip Came Out For Good Soup* (kingdom, phylum, class, order, family, genus, species) or *My Very Educated Mother Just Served Us Nine Pizzas* (Mercury, Venus, Earth,

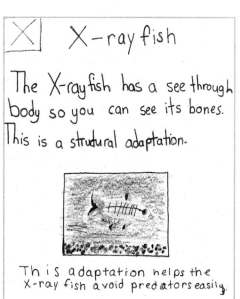

❱ **FIGURE 3.9**

Mars, Jupiter, Saturn, Uranus, Neptune, Pluto) in order to help remember key science information. (Of course, because of Pluto's demotion, *Nine Pizzas* became *Nachos.*) By creating the images in our mind, we create links with the content we are hoping to learn and memorize. This can be especially helpful with ELLs.

We can also use mnemonic cues to help us remember individual science terms. The keyword method (Atkinson 1975) is a versatile strategy that works in that manner. The method can visually reinforce a wide range of information. Students might want to remember scientific terms and their definitions, or perhaps the names of human organs and the functions of the organs in the body, or valuable minerals and the location where we can find the minerals. While you might want to create an example to model the strategy with a class, your students will remember more if they develop an image themselves because the image will have meaning to them. Figure 3.10 is an example of how a student might use the keyword method to learn the term *temperate.* (A reproducible of the form is available in Appendix F.)

A student begins by listing a science term, such as *temperate*, in the top left part of the paper and then listing a keyword, or a term visually similar to the term he or she is learning, in the top right side. In Figure 3.10, the term *temperature* is the keyword. Then the student lists the information to remember. In this case, it is a definition for the term. Finally, the student draws an illustration that incorporates both the keyword and the information to learn. Here, we see an illustration of two extreme weather conditions. In the middle, where the student shows the temperature is not extremely hot or cold, we see the figure smiling, flowers growing, and the sun shining. The weather looks neither too hot nor too cold; it is temperate.

By creating these images, our students remember information and create links with the content. Their pictures have a purpose because they help students to remember science terms and, therefore, serve as tools to develop scientific understanding.

Getting Our Students to Read Widely

While it is great to be knowledgeable about ideas for strengthening scientific vocabulary and emphasizing word relationships through motivating activities, I

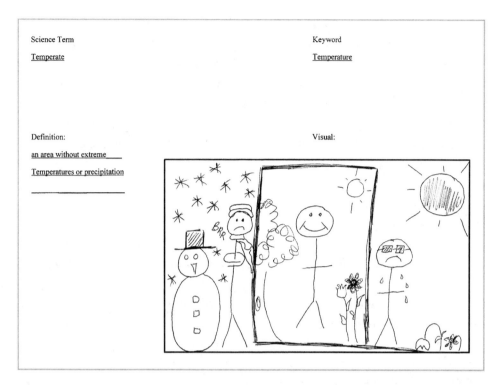

Science Term

Temperate

Keyword

Temperature

Definition:

an area without extreme

Temperatures or precipitation

Visual:

◀ FIGURE 3.10

believe the best way to develop students' scientific vocabulary is to simply get our students reading more texts on scientific topics. We know that the more students read, the more words they will encounter and the more proficient readers they will become (Vacca and Vacca 2005). Therefore, the more scientific texts our students read, the more scientific vocabulary terms they will encounter and learn. It sounds simple, but we have to find ways to encourage our students to seek out and read diverse scientific texts.

Science Text Talks

We know that peers often have a strong influence on students, so let's take advantage of that peer influence by having students share scientific reading material they enjoy through science text talks. Many language arts teachers use book talks to hook students on books. The five-minute talks are often just enough to interest students in reading a text. This can work for science too.

Begin by selecting a text that relates to the current science topic students are studying. This text might be an article on a website, a recently published trade book, a rap, or even a video on the topic. (Ideas for selecting texts are shared in Chapter 2.) Then model an effective three- to five-minute text talk on the text that will capture their interest in the book.

After your model talk, discuss what makes an effective text talk. Brainstorm the type of information students think other students want to hear, because there is nothing worse than listening to endless book reports or having students read off 3-by-5-inch cards on which they copied sentences from the jacket of a text or a website. What do their classmates *really* want to know? Why is the text interesting? What features really stand out in the text? Was there anything that made them want to keep reading? Why is the text worthy of recommendation to their peers? If they were awarding ratings, on a scale of 1–10, what rating should the text receive?

Ask a few students to each locate an interesting text on the science topic they are currently exploring and to prepare a brief three-minute scientific text talk. If possible, record the talks for students to listen to again later. Encourage the students who are listening to ask questions about the text. Is there more information they want to know about the text? Does this text relate to something they recently read? Involving the audience will make the science text talks valuable for all students.

Before Moving On

As this chapter shows, vocabulary instruction must play a very important role in our science classrooms. Our students encounter an unbelievably large number of new terms in science, and there must be strategies in place to determine not only the meaning of these terms but also future terms they may encounter. By drawing our students' attention to morphemes, emphasizing relationships between scientific concepts, developing word consciousness, and encouraging wide reading, we can strengthen their scientific vocabulary. Our ultimate goal is to develop students who can independently understand scientific information and add to their scientific knowledge base. In the next chapter, we will take a look at the unique demands of comprehending this scientific information and how we can assist our students with this process.

4

. . . .

Comprehending
Scientific Text

Think about the last time you read an informational book or a manual pertaining to an unfamiliar topic. You probably didn't have much prior knowledge to draw upon, so you read more slowly, focusing much more closely on
gaining meaning from the words present. You probably read and reread some
parts of the text in order to comprehend the information.

Our students often don't realize that all of us, including adults, encounter
text we don't understand, and this is often informational text on an unfamiliar topic. As adults, with years of reading experience, we have a repertoire of
strategies for understanding what we read, whether we use them consciously
or not. For example, more than likely we realize when we aren't understanding
something we read, and we reread it. We don't consciously think about it, but
we automatically do it because we have internalized the strategy. Our students

THINK ABOUT Looking Back on Elementary School

When you were a student in elementary school, what were the titles of some of your favorite books to read? Also, what books did adults in school share with you? What types of books were read aloud? Thinking about the categories of texts in Chapter 2, would you classify them as fictional, informational, hybrid, or poetry? How do you think reading or listening to these types of texts read aloud might or might not have had an impact on your understanding of content area material?

don't yet have the extensive experience we do with scientific text, and therefore we need to scaffold these strategies.

What makes comprehending science text so difficult for our students? Part of the difficulty is that science text is very different from the type of text our students are exposed to in the earlier grades. While there is an increasing emphasis on the importance of using informational text with younger students (Duke 2000; Pentimonti et al. 2010), most, if not all, of the students who walk through our classroom doors will be more familiar with narrative stories than informational text.

Developing Text Flexibility

More than likely, many of us remember listening to and reading a lot of fictional text during our elementary years. As young children hear folktales and other fables, they develop an understanding of the similarities the stories share. In fact, many young children immediately begin writing their own stories with "Once upon a time" and end them with "And they lived happily ever after" because students learn to expect that story structure. This knowledge of texts makes it easier for them to read other stories of the genre because they expect the structure, are familiar with some of the vocabulary terms, and have heard similar themes.

Unfortunately, students' knowledge of fictional stories does not necessarily lead to a better understanding of informational text. While there are

NOTICE HOW EXPERIENCED READERS READ INFORMATIONAL TEXT

Imagine that the principal walks into your classroom after school one day and hands you an informational text on an unfamiliar educational issue that she wants teachers to consider. The principal tells you that next week's faculty meeting will include a discussion of key points in the text. The principal wants each teacher to share a few ideas that he or she believes are important in the book. What immediately goes through your mind? Jot down on a sheet of paper the steps you would take to prepare for the faculty meeting. When you complete the list, look at what you wrote. How would you prepare for the faculty meeting? Would you skim through the text while watching a movie on the television and then put the text away until the meeting? Would you perhaps read it multiple times? Would you skim the text and then read through it more closely? Would you write notes, highlight, skim material, or discuss the content with a colleague? Would you try to organize your thoughts so that they would make sense to the rest of your audience (the other teachers)? Does the way you would approach the text depend on the type of text and your purpose for reading it?

Now, let's think about the struggling readers we have in our science classrooms. If they are given a similar request, which requires determining key points in a scientific text to share with other students, will they have ideas for handling such a request? Will they approach the reading differently than they would a graphic novel a friend showed them at lunch? Are students aware that they must think about the type of text and the purpose for reading? After thinking about these questions, write down on the paper three to five ways to help students gain information from a science text. Ask a colleague the same questions and share with each other what you wrote. See if you gain additional ideas for helping struggling readers that you might not have thought of before. ✱

benefits to reading and listening to fictional texts, we must continue to expand our students' text schema, or background knowledge, so that they know how to approach a wide variety of texts. Students need to realize that they must approach reading informational texts in a very different manner than reading narrative texts. Informational text contains a great deal of information and it often has features not found in fictional texts, such as a table of contents, a glossary, headings, and visuals. Unless our students are able to comprehend informational text, they will not be able to develop the content knowledge necessary to think like a scientist.

When we read nonfiction, our purpose for reading is very different than when we read narrative: we are looking to gain information, not get involved in a story. Students need to be aware that the way they approach text, or the stance they take, must vary depending on their purpose for reading (Rosenblatt 1938). I like to think of this as text flexibility. This means that students think about their purpose for reading as soon as they engage with a text and understand the demands associated with it.

Comprehending Like a Scientist

While our students encounter text throughout their lives, we know that informational text, and more specifically science text, has its own unique demands. Not only must students understand the differing demands of narrative and informational text, but they must realize that in order to think like a scientist they must understand the comprehension demands that scientists experience (Shanahan and Shanahan 2008). Scientific reading requires that the reader have a deep understanding of a large number of technical terms (see Chapter 3), is able to visualize what is read, understands how to shift between words and images (see Chapter 5), and has a familiarity with texts written with varying structures and for different purposes.

There are five key principles that can guide comprehension instruction so that our students think like scientists and comprehend texts written for various purposes and with different structures:

» Use and understand text features.
» Pay attention to the author's purpose.
» Focus on specific content.
» Engage with multiple texts on a scientific topic.
» Learn to support opinions with textual evidence.

Let's take a closer look at how these five comprehension guidelines can foster our students' scientific understanding.

Make the Most of Text Features

If you compare a science informational text and a fictional story, poem, or hybrid text, one of the most obvious differences is that the scientific text contains many text features not found in most hybrid or fictional texts: a table of contents, an index, or a glossary, perhaps, as well as features such as headings, captions, and specific use of fonts. Online informational texts also have unique features, such as sidebars and hyperlinks.

While it may seem obvious to us as experienced readers that these features help us to make sense of a scientific text's content, we can't assume that students are aware of their purpose. For example, we know that a heading tells the reader the main idea for a section of text, but students may need help understanding this feature. Students may also not know how to use a table of contents or electronic sidebar to see the organization of the information (or why it would be important to do so) or how to use an index to locate key information. There are many ways we can help our students to think about these features and learn to use them to better understand scientific text.

Take a Text Walk

Ask students to brainstorm a list of informational text features that they see in scientific text. As they share ideas, list those features on a large sheet of chart paper. Chances are that students will list many of the features included in Figure 4.1. Of course students may not list all of the features in Figure 4.1 or

appendix	graphs/charts	maps and keys
captions	headings/subheadings	sidebars
electronic menus	hyperlinks	table of contents
flowcharts	icons	tables
fonts	index	time lines
glossary	labeled diagrams	

◀ FIGURE 4.1

even be familiar with some of them, but the figure can provide ideas for features we might want to draw our students' attention to in scientific text.

Now invite students to take a text walk through an unfamiliar chunk of science text. This text can be a digital text or a traditional print text. As students look through their chunk of text, what informational text features do they see? Which of the features in their text are on the class list? They might even note the page numbers where they find the features to make it easier to share their findings with the rest of the class. Are there any text features they want to add to the list?

Ask students to think about why the author might have chosen to use the text features students identified. For example, perhaps there is a text box on the page that contains directions for an experiment, or maybe part of the text is italic. The text box may be there to help the reader realize that the chunk of text reads differently than the rest of the text or needs to be read separately from the main ideas of the text. Italics might bring attention to definitions of terms that the author thinks are important for the reader to know.

The next step is to have students work in small groups to examine a scientific text the class will be reading. This again can be any type of text. It might be a chapter or a lengthy article. Assign each group of students a specific range of pages to skim for informational text features. Their goal is to use the information they get from the text features on their text walk to create questions they expect to be able to answer as they read the text. For example, there may be a subheading, "Food Plays an Important Role in the Daily Life of a Seabird." Students might create questions such as, "What do seabirds eat?" or "Why is getting food such an important part of their daily life?" (Obviously food is important to everyone's existence, but if this is a subheading, there must be something unique about the eating habits of seabirds.) As a class, go through each section of text in order and have the students share their questions for those pages. Create a list of the questions for the class. Then have students go ahead and read the text. As they read, have them stop after each chunk to see if they can answer the questions using information from the text.

Read Like a Writer

We can introduce students to the idea of textual features by pointing out their use in day-to-day living. I know I even use a few textual features when I create

ANALYZE INFORMATIONAL TEXT FEATURES IN TRADE BOOKS

Thinking ahead to the next science topic you will teach, gather some informational science texts that you plan to share with students. Then photocopy the Informational Text Features Chart (Appendix G), and use the chart to review three or four of the scientific texts. Which of the informational text features on the list will students encounter in the texts? Will they see many of the features or only a few of them? If students will not see some of the features, note this so that you make sure to include texts with those features in other science units you study. The Informational Text Features Chart can help to ensure that you expose your students to a wide variety of text features commonly seen in scientific texts. ✱

my to-do list each week. I put the days of the week in a column going down the left-hand side of the paper, skipping a little space between each date. Why do I do this? Well, can you imagine trying to read a to-do list where everything was written in paragraph form? Features such as placement of text on the page make it easier to see at a glance what needs to be done. Also, let's think about a set of directions that we might get with a toaster oven, a scooter, or even a new cell phone. Don't the instructions use font size and type, visuals, and headings to make the material easier to understand?

Let's then ask our students to read like a writer. For just a few minutes, we want them to put themselves in the place of the author. As students reexamine a piece of scientific text they recently read, ask questions such as these:

1. What informational text features do you see in the text? Why do you think the author chose to use the informational text features that we see in this text? (Was the author trying to draw attention to specific information?)

2. Why do you think the author chose to structure the text the way it is? (For example, directions for experiments are often written so that there are not a lot of excess words. They are succinct, to the point, and often must be read sequentially. By contrast, a scientific article may contain paragraphs of information about each important point.)

3. Is there anything unique in this text that the author did to get the reader's attention? If so, what is it? (Sometimes an author may use color or a change in font to draw the reader's eye to a specific hyperlink or heading.)

Our purpose with this brief activity is to get students to reexamine a familiar scientific text from a perspective they may not otherwise consider. Authors use features for a reason, and by reading like a writer, our students are beginning to think about how scientific texts might vary and why an author might choose to convey information in a specific way.

As we focus our students' attention on informational text features they see in scientific text, we are helping to provide the key they need to unlock the scientific information within the text. While it isn't possible to use this strategy in its entirety on a regular basis because of the time constraints within our classrooms, we can use the chart in Figure 4.1 as an anchor chart so that students can refer back to the text features on the list as they engage with future texts. In this way, students will begin to make a habit of noticing and thinking about text features as they read future scientific texts.

Pay Attention to Purpose

Informational science text can serve many purposes. It may be written to inform, but it can also be written to persuade the reader to react in a specific way. In order for our students to comprehend science texts, they must understand that the author's purpose for writing the piece will affect the content and the presentation of the information within the text. Authors who are writing to persuade may focus on only one side of a scientific issue or they may draw attention to specific findings that support their view.

Many of our students believe that what they see in print is fact. Research shows that students often resist questioning ideas they see in text (Beck and McKeown 1988). This is partly because of the prominent role textbooks play in most classrooms. The textbook's authority in curriculum discourages students from questioning it (Luke, DeCastell, and Luke 1983). We have to teach our students that textbooks they encounter are "merely someone's words" (McKeown, Beck, and Worthy 1993, 562), and this really applies to all texts our students encounter in science. Reading without questioning anything in

LEARN TO EVALUATE INTERNET SOURCES

Unfortunately, many students believe that everything they read on the Internet is true. If this is an issue in your science classroom, consider discussing the following text with students: *But I Read It on the Internet* (Buzzeo 2013). It is an engaging trade book for students addressing the importance of both evaluating and citing sources. ✱

a text doesn't create a very deep level of understanding. It mainly provides our students with the ability to restate what they read because they are passively consuming the information on the page without thinking about other views on the topic, other information they may have read, or even how it ties to prior knowledge. Students should never see a text as having *the* answer. Instead our students need to use texts in the same way scientists use text. Scientists question and think about what they read. They examine other scientists' writing to help them with their own writing, to compare information in multiple sources, and to see how their own findings fit with those of others in the field (Yore 2004).

We have to get our students to question what they read if we want them to think at a higher level. The ability to question text requires that our students engage with the ideas present in the text and realize that the author doesn't have the ultimate power over the information the reader gains from the text. We want our students not to take the words at face value, but instead to think about the information and how it relates to other scientific information.

Thanks to technology, the amount of text available for our students to view is exponentially increasing, and often the texts students view through technology aren't subject to the same rigorous reviews as the traditional texts our students encounter in print. Just about anyone can post information very quickly for millions to see and share instantly across social media. While peer-reviewed articles that are repeatedly cited in top journals are often seen as seminal pieces, many online articles that are repeatedly shared may just be repeating misinformation. Therefore, students need to put scientific text *under the microscope* and look closely at its contents.

Looking Through the Lens at Science Text

We can begin by giving each student a copy of the chart shown in Figure 4.2. (available in Appendix H as a full-size reproducible). As students look over the chart, ask them why it's important to question what we see in print. The obvious reason is that sometimes people write information that isn't accurate, or the authors may want the reader to react or believe in a certain way. What do we know or what background information can we find about the author? Is the author a member of a specific organization that might gain by publishing the text? If so, we can keep that in mind as we read the text. If we can find information on the author's background, we might also have a good idea of whether or not the person is knowledgeable about the topic.

We also want to pay attention to the type of text and its presentation. Most publishers have a strict review process for their authors prior to publishing a text. However, if it is a digital text or a press release, does the text have the same rigorous review? Does the author use emotional terms to grab the reader's attention? Is attention drawn to certain information through images, the use of color, or other means? Is the author presenting only one side of an argument? Finally, even if scientific information is factual, it may be that the text is not up-to-date and so the information is no longer accurate. When did the author publish the text, and does that cause the reader to question the information in the piece?

After students review the chart, give them an article or short text from a print source or the Internet. Have the students work in groups to complete the first column. Then bring the class back together to discuss students' responses. What were they able to determine about the author's purpose, the type of text, and any potential bias?

After completing and talking through the first column with a teacher-supplied text, students can locate and bring in two more examples of texts pertaining to the scientific topic. Encourage them to bring in a variety of texts. Students might bring articles from the Internet, trade books, simulations, and so on. Have them work either individually or in groups to complete the rest of the chart using the texts they chose.

After students complete the chart, discuss with the class how the questions on the chart have shaped their reactions to the texts. Did they question

---

APPENDIX H   Looking Through the Lens

Scientists love to take a closer look at things by viewing them through a microscope's lens. Let's take a closer look at scientific texts by also Looking Through the Lens at them. Write down the titles of three texts on a topic at the bottom of the page. Then think about *each* of the questions under the Areas to Analyze. Jot your notes in the correct column. What did you learn about the texts?

Areas to Analyze	Text 1	Text 2	Text 3
Reason: Why was this science text written? Did the author want to entertain/persuade/inform?			
Type of Science Text: Is this a digital text or a printed text? Is this a brochure, article, press release, or some other type of text?			
Important Details: Are important details included? What text features were used? Are there emotional words used to persuade or show bias?			
Source: Who wrote, illustrated, and published the piece? Do we know anything about the source?			
Time of Text Creation: Is this piece current? If not, is there reason to question the accuracy of the information?			

Text 1: _____

Text 2: _____

Text 3: _____

◀ FIGURE 4.2

any information they read, or did any sources appear to provide more accurate information than others? What made them value scientific information in one source over that in another source? Did they read some of the texts differently than others after finding out information about the author or perhaps realizing that the author had a bias on the topic?

While it isn't realistic to expect students to fill out the chart for every text they encounter, they can refer to the questions on it as they read on their own.

With practice, they will internalize the questions. You might have them staple a copy of the chart in the back of their science journal. As students encounter texts throughout the year, refer them back to the chart so that they think about the source of the scientific information they are reading.

Focus Attention on Content

Scientific text has a lot of important information within it. Therefore, our students have to learn to read and remember specific information they gain from the text. Not only do they have to take into consideration informational text features, but they also must have the metacognitive awareness to monitor their understanding of scientific content. We can scaffold our students' understanding so that they develop this metacognitive awareness and are able to independently monitor their comprehension of future scientific text.

Text Annotations

One way to encourage students to think about what they are reading in science is through annotating text. For this activity, you want to provide short scientific articles or photocopies of selections from longer texts on which students can write. In order to be able to refer to specific areas of the text later, number each paragraph on the text. You can use this activity with an entire class or with a small group of struggling readers so that the students internalize how "good" readers approach text.

Begin by thinking about your students' observations and class discussions. What specific aspects of text are presenting issues and creating misunderstanding for students? Are students having trouble stating the main idea of what they're reading? Are they monitoring their understanding and stopping to ask questions if they don't understand the text? Perhaps you want students to locate words that they feel they need to know to understand the passage or maybe draw conclusions from the text. Annotating text can serve as a way to focus on any of these issues. The benefit of annotation is that students actively engage with material as their attention is drawn to not only the content but also the structure of the text (Zywica and Gomez 2008).

Next, ask students about the type of information they believe can help them to more easily understand scientific text they read. What creates confusion as they read? Perhaps they feel it might be valuable to notate unfamiliar words they encounter or questions they have as they read or to mark the main idea of text sections. Perhaps they have experience with this kind of annotation from their language arts classes and can share ideas from that experience. As a class, create a chart with some of the key items students might mark in the text and ideas for how students might mark the text. Figure 4.3 provides ideas for the types of information students might annotate and symbols they might use to annotate the information. Depending on the students' grade level and experience, it may be helpful to limit the various types of items students initially annotate in the text.

To introduce the idea of annotation, explain that students will be reading through the first page or two of the science text together. Pass out a copy of the text to each student and place the first page of the text under the document

IDEAS FOR ANNOTATING SCIENCE TEXT

What to Look For	How to Mark It
1. **Fact:** I think this is an important fact I want to remember!	F (and arrow pointing to fact)
2. **Visual:** This visual is an important part of the text!	V
3. **Key Science Term:** This is a science word we learned in class.	Triangle
4. **Confusion:** I don't understand this part of the text.	??
5. **Connection:** This reminds me of something else I learned in science.	C = other connection
6. **Heading/Subheading:** This heading or subheading helps me to understand the text.	Circle
7. **Unfamiliar Word:** I don't know this word and can't figure it out from the text.	?W
8. **Main Idea:** This sounds like the main idea of the text.	Underline

◀ FIGURE 4.3

camera. Read through the first page as a class, and draw students' attention to the class chart. What information do they want to annotate on the text? As students mark and orally share items, make the notes on the class copy of the text using the document camera. At the end of the first page, talk about their markings. If students are marking unfamiliar scientific terms, what strategies can they use to better understand specific terms they choose to mark? Can they look at the context or other information the author provides to get an idea of their meaning? Do they need to consider looking up the unfamiliar words in a dictionary?

Let students continue reading the next couple of pages as they individually annotate. Then bring the class back together to discuss what they annotated. As they become more familiar with the annotation process, there may be other items not shown in Figure 4.3 that the students might suggest to annotate or even areas you feel could benefit from their focus. The number of items to annotate may increase as students become more comfortable with this strategy and think of other areas to annotate. However, the number of items is just as likely to decrease because as students annotate additional areas, they will internalize some strategies and no longer need to annotate those items.

As teachers, we need to think about what we want our students to do when they finish annotating a chunk of text because annotation doesn't need to be the end of our students' learning. Perhaps students can jot key vocabulary terms in their science journals. If students note questions they have as they read the text, can those questions be the focus of small-group discussions?

Of course it isn't realistic to write on all types of text, and we can't continue to indefinitely photocopy texts. In order to continue this activity on other types of print text, students can jot any questions they have about the science text, confusing terms they encounter, or key points they want to remember on sticky notes. Even then, though, we know as good readers we do not tend to write a lot of notes on the scientific texts we read. While we might note an important point occasionally, most of us internalize the process of noticing key terms, drawing conclusions, and noticing key information. Our goal for annotating text is for our students to begin noticing these types of information in scientific text and to gradually internalize the process so that they are not writing and using sticky notes. Through introducing the idea of annotation,

THINK ABOUT Asking Students to Annotate Text
· ·
Let's think about a couple of key considerations regarding student annotation: Should all students' annotations look the same? No, they shouldn't. We want students to annotate text in ways that are meaningful to them. How do we want student annotation to impact their reading of scientific text? Our goal is to have students slow down as they pay more attention to key elements and reread text so that their comprehension improves. What are your goals for your students? How might annotation help them?

modeling with our students, and gradually removing the scaffolds, we'll help our students be better able to understand scientific content they encounter.

3-2-1 Strategy

We can also use the 3-2-1 strategy (Zygouris-Coe, Wiggins, and Smith 2004) as a quick way for students to summarize what they learn in science. It is also an excellent discussion starter and can help our students comprehend scientific text. While the initial strategy focuses on restating learning or ideas students comprehend, it can also help students create connections between texts and science experiences.

After our students complete a science experiment, view a simulation, or participate in a field trip, they can use this strategy to tie learning back into scientific text on the topic. After the hands-on activity, ask students to write down *three* interesting facts they were able to learn during the experience, *two* ways they can connect the information back to scientific text they are reading or recently read on the topic, and *one* question they still have about the topic.

While the facts they write down require that they reflect on their learning, the two connections ensure that our students are comprehending the scientific text they are reading. In addition, creating these connections enables them to see how scientific information ties together. Finally, the question they still have about the topic can give them a purpose for reading other scientific text.

After students have time to write down their responses to the three parts of this strategy, ask them to share some of the interesting facts they found. Discuss connections they were able to make between their experiences and scientific text. Finally, ask students to share the questions they still have about the topic. Do they think they will find the answers to the questions later in the unit? If they are unsure, can other students in the class think of a way to find answers to any of the questions? You can then group together students who have similar questions so that they can seek out answers in scientific texts.

By sharing their writing and clarifying the statements, our students expand their scientific thinking and may correct misconceptions. For example, students may not accurately comprehend text, and therefore, the connections may be inaccurate. Or perhaps they have a question after the science experience, but other students believe that the information is in the science text recently read. Students can go back into the text to determine if they misunderstood any part of the text. An important component of this strategy is the discussion that ensues.

Figure 4.4 shows how one teacher used the strategy after students dissected a chicken. There was a lot of excitement in the room during the chicken dissection, so in order to settle the class back down and debrief, the teacher asked the students to complete a 3-2-1 activity. The students each gave three interesting findings from the dissection. Then the teacher had them find two ways the information they learned from the dissection connected to material they had previously read. Finally, she had them state one question they wanted to explore further on the topic. Figure 4.4 contains one student's response to the 3-2-1 activity.

In the example in Figure 4.4, the student tied the information from the dissection to two different texts that the class was reading. While this student was able to write the information in paragraph form for each part of the strategy, younger students or ELLs may choose to simply list the facts, connections, and question each in a sentence.

Gerard

12-1
7SA

Chicken leg dissection

During the dissection, I learned that the leg had an insane amount of protection & skin on top of it. I found it very interesting how strong the layers were on top of the bone. It took my partner and I quite a while to pull off the skin. I was also suprised at the amount of fat there was on the bone.

This dissection connects to Chapter 7 in our review book, because on pg 199 it talks about the skeletal system and how hard the bones are. In the dissection, we felt the bones + joints. It also talks obout the cartilage, which we felt also. It also refers to pg 198 because it includes all the blood, bones, muscle and skin. During the dissection, we touched the bones + muscle and blood was all over my hands. I also pulled off a bunch of skin.

This dissection also connects to ch. 15 in our science text book, on pg 445. The page teaches about the bone tissue and cartilage. During the dissection, I felt the cartilage + the bone tissue. It also talks about the structure of the bone which we observed up close.

I learned so much from the dissection, but I am still curious about why fat is needed on our bodies or the chicken's leg.

◀ FIGURE 4.4

Text-Dependent Questions

Another way to help students focus on key content is through thoughtful examination of the questions we ask students about what they read. Through effective questioning, we can engage students with science text and develop their
ability to use text to support their statements and opinions, an area of emphasis
in both the CCSS and the NGSS. The ELA CCSS require middle school students
to cite specific information from a science or technical text, share the conclusions from the text without adding in their prior knowledge or other information, analyze why the author included specific information, and examine the
structure of the science or technical text (RST 6-8.1 to 6-8.5).

To help students learn to support their answers with evidence from text, we
must ask questions that require students to use information found in scientific
texts. Fisher and Frey (2012) talk about six types of text-dependent questions:

» **General Understandings:** These questions are broader by nature, requir-
ing students to give the overall idea or the gist of the material.

» **Key Details:** Remember the five Ws (who, what, why, where, and
when)? Those Ws can help students provide the details that lead to general understanding.

» **Vocabulary and Text Structure:** These questions, like those in the
activities in the previous chapter, focus on the specific terms readers
see in the text and the way the material is written. If a scientific piece
of writing is a letter to the editor, does the author use specific terms to
persuade or change others' views? If we are comparing two texts on the
same scientific topic, what do we notice about the format each author
chose to use?

» **Author's Purpose:** These questions focus on the reason the author
wrote the piece, and how that might impact the information within the
text. Have students think about how others might have written differently on the topic. (Refer to some of the activities earlier in this chapter
that focus on the author's purpose.)

» **Inferences:** What conclusions can the reader draw from the information in the text? Can students support the assumptions they make with
textual referents?

» **Opinions, Arguments, and Intertextual Connections:** To answer these questions, students state their opinions and support them with textual information, and they also make connections with previous material they read on the topic or information they gained from other sources such as experiments or other hands-on experiences. (I'll talk more about this later.)

See Figure 4.5 for examples of each type of text-dependent question related to an informational text, *Bicycles Roll In* (National Science Resources Center 2006a), which shares how bicycles have changed over time. This brief text was part of a unit on motion and design that looked at the invention of various types of vehicles and the designs behind them.

SCIENTIFIC TEXT-DEPENDENT QUESTIONS ABOUT EXCERPT FROM *BICYCLES ROLL IN* (National Science Resources Center 2006a)

General Understandings: How has the design of bicycles changed over time?

Key Details: Who is the creator of the velocipede? What came after the velocipede?

Vocabulary and Text Structure: If you compare this text with *The Mechanics of Bikes* (National Science Resources Center 2006b), what are some obvious differences between the way the information is presented in each? What does the term *mechanics* refer to?

Author's Purpose: Why were the two pieces written?

Inferences: Which type of bicycle discussed would be the safest to ride and why? If you own a bicycle, does it have a derailleur, and how do you know?

Opinions, Arguments, and Intertextual Connections: Thinking back to other types of transportation that we have read about and considering when the other types of transportation were developed, why or why not would the bicycle have been considered an important invention? How does what we learned about friction tie into the information on bicycles?

◀ FIGURE 4.5

The six categories of questions can help us to rethink how we engage our students with scientific text. We know that our students cannot read scientific text in the same way they read other types of text, and by ensuring we use a variety of text-dependent questions when we talk about text in the classroom, we are encouraging our students to approach scientific text in a way that will help them to better comprehend what they are reading. Whether students are working with partners to review research findings on a topic, interacting in small groups to examine multiple texts on a topic, or independently reading a digital text, we can facilitate student comprehension by ensuring that they are answering these types of questions.

Engage with Multiple Texts

Another important skill our students need to develop is the ability to critically read and comprehend across a variety of texts. The ability to synthesize information they find in diverse texts will be vital not only for students' future careers but for them to be successful throughout their lives. For example, if I decide to plant a vegetable garden, want to know about age-appropriate activities I can do with my son during vacation, or have questions about a particular disease my elderly dog may have, I am not going to be content to google an online source, talk to an expert, or get a nonfiction text on the topic. While one of those texts may be a start to my research, I am going to want to consult multiple texts that pertain to the topic. These texts may include simulations, multimodal texts, informational texts, YouTube videos, or other sources. As good readers, we can usually read multiple texts and discern important information, but our students often need practice and structure to comprehend multiple texts on the same topic.

Engaging with multiple texts requires our students to be able to synthesize the information they get from numerous sources in order to find the central idea and conclusions. It isn't enough for our students to know what each source says about a topic; students have to also be able to draw a conclusion from the texts as a whole. Therefore, we have to expose our students to diverse texts so that they are familiar with the variety of ways authors can structure and convey scientific information. As the definition of text continues to change, we need to ensure that we prepare our students to not only understand the texts but to analyze and synthesize the information within.

THINK ABOUT THE QUESTIONS YOU ASK IN SCIENCE

Record one of your science lessons, or work with a colleague to visit and observe each other's classes. During that time, list the questions that students answer during the science class. Afterward, look at the list and ask yourself: Are the questions primarily text-independent or text-dependent questions? Do the questions represent each of the six types of questions Fisher and Frey describe? How could I modify or ask additional questions to ensure that my students will comprehend scientific texts? You might want to repeat this activity at different points during the year to see if there is a change in the types of questions you're asking. The goal is to make sure that text-dependent questions play a key role in classroom activities. ✱

Synthesizing Information

One way we can encourage our students to examine multiple texts and synthesize the information they find is through the use of Manderino's multiple gist strategy (2007). This strategy encourages the use of diverse texts (e.g., visuals, websites, and textbooks) as students seek to determine the *gist* of texts. However, we can also use this strategy to incorporate information our students gain not only from trade books or digital texts but also from local texts (see Chapter 2) our students create from hands-on science lessons or even field trips.

After students experience a hands-on science experiment or take a field trip, divide the class into small groups of students. If students work in pairs to complete a science experiment, each pair may create a group by working together with another pair of students. The next step is to ask each of the small groups to look over and discuss their science notes. They are then going to write a summary, or the gist, of their notes. Since you don't want your students to write down every detail but primarily the main idea of the information, it works best to tell students that they are going to turn over their science notes when they write the gist of the information they have read. Typically students use about twenty words to write their gist. I usually find that twenty words works well with a short piece of text. It challenges our students, but it isn't so difficult that they can't complete the writing.

After each group of students creates a gist, ask each small group to share its summary with the rest of the class. Discuss how the summaries are similar or different. Was the task difficult? If so, what made it challenging? How do students decide what information to keep or leave out?

Now, invite students to look at other chunks of text pertaining to the topic they are studying. Encourage them to explore simulations, multimedia texts, informational trade books, or even videos pertaining to the science topic. As students explore each text, encourage them to come together as small groups to write a new twenty-word summary that synthesizes the new information they have learned with the information from the previous science experience. While you can continue this activity with multiple science texts, it's often necessary to allow students to use a larger number of words for the summary as the number of texts they read increases. This might mean using thirty to forty words to summarize scientific texts. Once again ask students to share their final gist. What did they accomplish by completing the activity? Discuss how they were able to look at a great deal of information and determine the main idea. Also, discuss that synthesizing information into a succinct main idea is a valuable skill, but there are also times when they will want to be able to cite specific details.

Support Opinions with Text

We all know from the moment children can speak that they have opinions, and often these are pretty darn strong opinions. They can't wait to share their opinions regarding information they hear, rules they have to follow, or even suggestions from parents or peers. However, while our students are more than likely ready and willing to share their opinions, we have to work with our students if we want them to learn to support their opinions like a scientist. Scientists can't just state their views. Instead they must support their statements with factual information. Therefore, we have to teach our students the importance of supporting scientific statements with facts.

Marking an Opinion on a Continuum

One way we can help our students to practice supporting their opinions is through a modification of the popular strategy polar opposites (Bean and Bishop

1992). This strategy requires that a student reads a statement and then marks his or her view on a continuum. As students orally share their views, they go back into the text to cite specific information that supports their choices. We can also use polar opposites to encourage students to seek out additional information in texts to support their opinions and to include written citations from those texts.

To begin with, create three to five statements on a scientific topic with polar opposite answers for students to consider. For example, if you were studying cancer, you might create three to five statements similar to the following one:

Cancer is:

preventable _____ _____ _____ _____ _____ unpreventable

If you were discussing space travel in class, you might want to create three to five statements similar to the following:

We should spend _____ money on space travel:

very little _____ _____ _____ _____ _____ a great deal

In order to encourage students to seek out diverse texts for answers, the statements should not have a single, specific answer. For example, there would be very little research necessary and very little discussion if you used the following statement for space travel:

Man landed on the moon for the first time in:

1965 _____ _____ _____ _____ 1970

With a statement like this one, students can very quickly find one source regarding the first moon landing in 1969, mark the space before 1970, and be done. That doesn't encourage a great deal of research, involve more than one citation to support the response, or include any opinions. We want our students to think deeply about science, so we want to create statements that cause them to look at more than one side of a topic and to explore the information that they find in text. While initially it may be easier for you to create the statements, as students gain experience with the strategy and understand its use, they can help to create the controversial statements to which they will seek answers.

Since students often have strong views, one option is to allow them to mark their opinions on the continuum prior to researching the topic. You can have students mark their views in pencil and then have them use pens to mark their opinions after they research the topic. While they might not think their opinions will change, the possibility exists! Sometimes once we know the facts about a topic, we realize that perhaps we want to change our views. This also shows our students the importance of gathering information before stating views.

Once students mark their initial views for each statement, ask them to examine two or more additional scientific texts that relate to the topic and then have them decide where on the continuum to place their final opinions. Each student should also state two or three facts from each source that influenced his or her choice. You can extend this activity by having each student review the facts he or she listed to support his or her opinion on the statement and synthesize the information from those sources to succinctly state the opinion in a few sentences.

This strategy is not just for texts. It could also be valuable after a science experiment, the viewing of a simulation, or a real or virtual field trip on a topic. Students can cite specific pages in their science journals or field trip notes as well as other texts they find on the topic.

Orally Sharing Support for an Opinion

Speed sharing is another great way for students to learn to use specific textual references to support their views on a science topic. Once students can support their views in writing with the polar opposite activity, we can encourage them to begin orally articulating their views with supporting textual evidence. It is more difficult to orally support an opinion when there is another person asking questions because students can't prepare for every question that their audience might ask.

Begin by choosing a topic in science that will evoke varying opinions. For example, you might ask your students whether or not they believe that individuals can make a significant difference in reducing environmental damage due to global warming. Then each student will state his or her view on the topic at the top of a sheet of paper (e.g., "I believe individuals can make a significant difference in regard to global warming."). Of course, this is a student's initial view, and each may decide to change his or her view before sharing with the class. The next step is to provide time for students to use various types of text to research information that supports their opinions (or, perhaps, that leads them to change their opinions). After they complete their research on the topic, have each student write approximately three to five support statements for his or her opinion on the same page, along with citations from the text that provide support for each statement. Once the students do this, it is time for the speed sharing to begin!

Have students place their chairs in two rows facing each other. If space is an issue, students can form two circles with their chairs so that every chair in the outer circle is facing a chair in the inner circle. Have the students sit in the chairs so that they each have a partner.

When it is time to start, students must take turns sharing their opinions and the reasons that support their views. Plan to provide a minute or so for each person to share with a partner. When that time is up, tell the pairs of students that they can now briefly ask their partners questions about their views. Because of the brief period of time, students have to stay on the topic or they won't be able to successfully complete the speed sharing.

When time is up, one row of students (or the smaller circle) stay in their chairs, and the other row (or those sitting in the outside circle) move one seat over so that everyone is now facing a new partner. Then students can repeat this exercise with new partners until everyone has a chance to share with five or more students.

With this strategy, it isn't important that two students with opposing views are always sharing with each other, but it is important that a diversity of views is present in the classroom so students can see how others were able to support a different viewpoint than theirs. After the speed sharing activity ends, bring the class back together and have a class discussion about the activity. What did students learn from the activity? Did any of the students change their opinions because of the evidence from a citation? Is there a way they might look at text differently so that they can better support their opinions? This class experience can easily lead to a writing activity because the ability to cite textual evidence helps students with persuasive writing.

Before Moving On

Helping our students to comprehend scientific texts they encounter is not an easy task. Scientific texts require our students to ask questions they may not typically think about when reading some other types of materials. With science texts, the author, the author's purpose, and the time of creation play key roles in how we think about what we are reading. We also have to use any information we can get from the textual features to better understand the text. Finally, we have to learn to examine, compare, and synthesize information from multiple scientific texts on the same topic and then be able to state our opinions with support from those texts.

As we think about the use of scientific text in our own classrooms, we can use the guidelines in this chapter to help frame how our students engage with scientific text. In that way, we can ensure that our students' ability to comprehend scientific information continues to develop. Of course there is still one other key aspect of scientific text that we must consider, and that is visuals. The next chapter will examine how we can help our students to understand the many visuals they encounter in the science classroom.

5

Taking a Good Look at Images in Science

When I read textbooks as a student, and came to images (e.g., graphs, charts, diagrams) in my textbook, I would skip those pages. I felt as if I had one less page to read, and the image wasn't that important. I assumed any important information would be in the words. Many students feel the same way about images. In fact, research shows that students often skip over images since they believe that images often restate what is in the written text or the images are primarily in the text to catch the reader's interest (Martins 2002). Unfortunately, if our students skip images, they are missing out on a lot of important information.

Science textbooks and other science texts for middle school students are seeing a significant increase in the amount of images (Lee 2008). Even more importantly, these images are much more complex than they were years ago, so skimming or skipping the images will result in students not thoroughly

ANALYZE YOUR USE OF IMAGES

Take ten minutes and jot down all of the images your students encounter in science class during a typical week. Do the types of images vary? Does the list include simulations, demonstrations, and videos?

If the list contains only images students traditionally encounter in print sources, how can you create additional opportunities for your students to strengthen their knowledge of other types of images? *

comprehending science content. We and our students also encounter images beyond those in print media. There are computer simulations, websites, PowerPoint presentations, videos, and other representations of information. Images are all around us.

While we often spend a great deal of energy in our classrooms helping our students strengthen their scientific vocabulary and better comprehend written scientific material, we must also focus our energy on helping students realize the power of images and how to interpret them.

Understanding the Unique Role Images Play in Science

Everyone encounters and engages with images on a daily basis whether he or she pursues a scientific career or not. These images can range from photographs friends share and the basic symbols used to denote restrooms at a restaurant to the weather maps that are shown on the news or graphs in articles we read. In addition, almost anything that we need to assemble comes with directions containing the written steps and accompanying images (or an online video) to help us complete the process. Images are everywhere in society.

While any adult encounters a wide range of images, including graphs and diagrams, scientists must engage with these more abstract forms of images on a routine basis. Often scientific reports and articles they read will contain images representing data or other technical information and possibly even labeled diagrams. According to Shanahan and Shanahan (2008), scientists must be able to weave back and forth between images and words in order to gain information.

They must be able to not only gain information from the abstract images but also determine how that information fits in with the accompanying text. This is an important skill that must be taught if students are going to be able to comprehend scientific material and be able to read like a scientist.

The Benefit of Using Images

Pretend for a moment that you are given two texts on a topic. One conveys everything through words, and the second text includes images. Which text is more appealing to read? I bet you would choose the one with images. Now, think about our students. They have spent a great deal of their lives encountering images on TV, in video games, and on many devices outside of school. Visual representations of information can be very motivating for students and can help connect unfamiliar scientific information through a familiar means. Images can present a great deal of information in a way that draws our attention to the material and makes it appear less formidable.

These images can also help our students to remember information (Treagust 2007). As our students focus on images, think about the scientific concepts, and try to understand the relationship between the information in the images and the written word, they will develop a more thorough understanding of the material and remember it. In fact, research suggests that using multimodal forms of teaching (e.g., information we encounter on computers, through videos, and in print sources) enables ELLs to make important connections to the content information present in the classroom (Ajayi 2009).

The Challenges of Using Images

I believe the initial challenge in using images is that often we consider images in general as less worthy than words. For example, even though many of us in education repeatedly emphasize the importance of picture books with students in the older grades, many people see those texts as less worthy texts or texts geared more for those who can't read as well. We have to rethink our view on images. We have to value images in the same way we value words, and we have to convey their importance to our students. According to Flood and Lapp (1998), we have an irrational loyalty to the printed word. That has to change. Our students will not be literate, and definitely not scientifically literate, unless

THINK ABOUT Taking into Consideration Students with
Visual Impairments

As we think about our students, we have to take into consideration the special needs of students with visual impairments. The large number of images in a science classroom can create additional challenges for those students. What are some ways we can modify the science curriculum to help those students be successful? We may need to enlarge images, or even use special devices so that they can view videos or samples under a microscope. The modifications will depend on the needs of the individual student.

they value the role images can play in conveying meaning. While the first books many of us look at as children are primarily or entirely composed of pictures, we have to realize that the complex images we read as adults are very different. These diagrams, charts, and graphs are not just simple add-ons to the content. Instead they often reinforce, organize, or even extend the information available in the words.

Another challenge is that our students need guidance in order to gain any potential advantages we associate with images. Merely exposing students to more images is not going to develop their knowledge of science content. In fact, images may actually confuse our students so that they learn less content from the text or perhaps gain misconceptions because of a misunderstanding about what an image is showing. If our students fail to understand the scale accompanying a map or inaccurately interpret a complex graph, they could misconstrue scientific information. Many texts provide minimal support to the reader, and over half of the images don't even include a label (Slough et al. 2010). Therefore, while the use of images can be beneficial with the teaching of science, this will be true only if we provide the support students need to understand the representations.

Strengthening Our Students' Knowledge of Images

As teachers, we know that it isn't enough to just point out images in scientific text or draw students' attention to them. We need to do a lot more than that. Our students will learn much more if we engage them with images they encounter in science through discussion and questioning and also if we teach students the best way to use images to represent their own scientific ideas (Hubber, Tytler, and Haslam 2010; Van Meter et al. 2006).

We can begin by keeping in mind three key principles, which should guide our instruction as students engage with images:

» Understand the purpose.
» Recognize the types.
» Comprehend information in images.

These three principles are essential if our students are going to be able to think, read, and write like scientists. First of all, they must realize the purpose images serve. Images may make text more visually engaging, restate information in a text, help organize the material, or add new information to the content. Students also must recognize the various types of images and their uses. If students can't understand the differences between graphs and labeled diagrams and appropriately refer to them, it is difficult, if not impossible, to talk about the various images students encounter and understand how the images vary. Students also cannot just absorb the information in images. Just as with words, our students need to understand that images require certain strategies in order to unlock the information they contain.

The Purpose of Images

Let's think about four purposes images serve in scientific text. Our students need to be aware that there is a reason that these images are part of the scientific text they are reading. For these four purposes, I'm adapting Levin's (1981) common categories of images that we find in science texts: decorative, representational, organizational, and extension.

Decorative Images

Decorative images don't provide any additional information about the science content with which our students are engaging. While this type of picture might initially catch the reader's interest, the reader learns nothing from the image itself. For example, if I want to create a poster listing the safety rules for science experiments, I might create a list containing five to ten brief rules. However, if I add an illustration of various science elements all around the borders of the figure, the illustration would serve as decoration because the images add no information to the topic. It's easy to remember this category because these images do little more than decorate or try to make the information on the page more appealing to our sense of sight, and yet these types of images can also negatively impact our understanding of text.

In fact, when researchers took a look at four sixth-grade science texts, they saw that one-third of the images in the texts were decorative (Slough et al. 2010). Therefore, even though our students won't gain information from these decorative pictures, it is important that they are aware of these images. If we don't provide guidance with images and talk about decorative pictures, this type of image may distract our students. It is easy for readers to miss entire chunks of information they are examining because their attention is drawn to the decorative picture and away from the content. We also have to think about images students create. When students create their own science projects, we want to encourage them to think about the type of images they include and to ensure that the images enhance the reader's understanding of the content instead of distracting the reader.

Representational Images

Representational images reinforce the scientific information that the words in the text provide. These types of pictures have the benefit that the text and images convey the information through two different symbol systems (words and pictures) so that our students actually view the information twice. This can be beneficial because students who learn better through images can see the presentation of information through that form while those who typically prefer reading words can engage with the content in that manner. Furthermore, everyone views the material in two ways, reinforcing the scientific content. Figure 5.1 is an example of a representational image. This example shows the labeled parts of an atom.

The words in the text actually tell us that there are protons, neutrons, and electrons within an atom. We also learn that the nucleus, which contains neutrons and protons, is in the center of the atom while the electrons swirl around the nucleus in an electron cloud. While the written words in the text convey the information, the symbols in the diagram reinforce the information in a visual form. When students choose to include pictures that restate information in the text during the creation of their own projects, they are demonstrating that they have a basic level of understanding of the scientific concepts because they are taking the information from one symbol system (words) and sharing it through another (images).

While these types of pictures are frequently seen in science texts at the upper grade levels, and students often choose

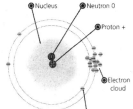

Parts of an Atom

All of the matter in the universe is made up of atoms—even your body. A human body is made up of about 7 billion billion BILLION atoms. About 67% of the atoms are hydrogen. Twenty-five percent of the atoms are oxygen. Hydrogen and oxygen atoms make up water, the most common substance in your body. Ten percent of the atoms in your body are carbon.

Atoms are made of **protons** (PROH tahnz), **neutrons** (NOO trahnz), and **electrons** (ih LEK trahnz).

Protons and neutrons are in an atom's nucleus. The **nucleus** is the center of an atom.

An atom usually has the same number of protons and neutrons. Neutrons add **mass** to an atom.

The electrons swirl around the nucleus. The area of the atom that contains the electrons is called the **electron cloud**. The number of electrons in an atom is usually the same as the number of protons.

If you could break hydrogen, oxygen, and carbon atoms apart, you would see that all of the protons, neutrons, and electrons are the same. How can you tell which atom is which? You need to count the number of protons.

◀ **FIGURE 5.1**

to create these images, we want to encourage students to realize that there are other purposes for images. If students feel as if images merely represent the information already in the text, they may assume that they don't need to closely examine images if they understand the text. After all, the images are just restating the scientific information. The remaining two categories of images challenge this perception.

Organizational Images

We often see images that organize the information our students encounter in written scientific text. It is very difficult to explain the steps of photosynthesis, the process of evaporation, and the stages of the life cycle of a frog without using an image that organizes the information. I immediately think about the power of an arrow. The use of arrows on images can take the place of so many words and also make information so much easier to understand.

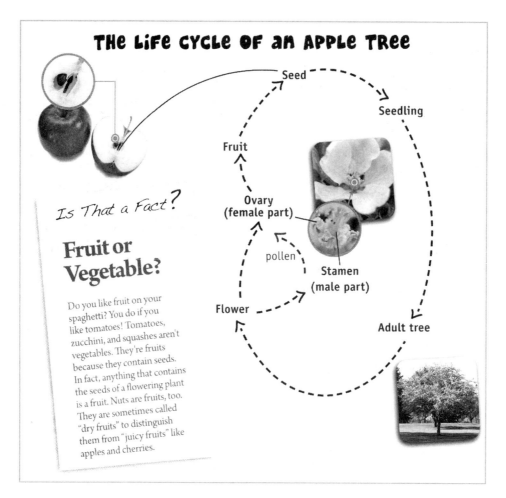

THE LIFE CYCLE OF AN APPLE TREE

Seed

Seedling

Fruit

Ovary
(female part)

pollen

Stamen
(male part)

Flower

Adult tree

Is That a Fact?

Fruit or Vegetable?

Do you like fruit on your spaghetti? You do if you like tomatoes! Tomatoes, zucchini, and squashes aren't vegetables. They're fruits because they contain seeds. In fact, anything that contains the seeds of a flowering plant is a fruit. Nuts are fruits, too. They are sometimes called "dry fruits" to distinguish them from "juicy fruits" like apples and cherries.

◀ FIGURE 5.2

The diagram in Figure 5.2 is an organizational image that explains the life cycle of an apple tree. In this picture, we see how an apple seed can ultimately result in a fruit. The arrows are used to show that a flower on an apple tree develops both male and female parts and to show how pollen is used to create the fruit. The publisher uses arrows to clarify the images.

Understanding or creating this type of picture requires a higher level of understanding than when dealing with either decorative or representational pictures. Decorative images add no scientific information and representational ones merely show what is in the text. However, organizational images show

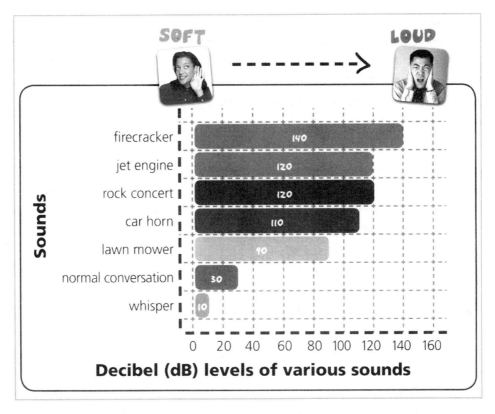

a process. Whether the process is demonstrating how birds take flight or how an animal changes with age, we have to be able to recognize the purpose of the symbols, such as arrows, and be able to visualize in our minds what is occurring.

Extension Images

Extension images go beyond what is in the text and provide additional information to the reader in an attempt to illustrate a complex scientific topic. They move beyond organizing the information available in the words. If our students skip these images, they are missing out on valuable information that adds to the text. Figure 5.3 is an example of an extension picture. While the text refers to amplitude and loudness and talks about the fact that we can measure sound in decibels, the image expands on that information by showing the range in decibels for a variety of sounds. The written words explain only that we measure sounds in decibels and that sounds beyond 120 decibels will damage a person's ears. The image goes beyond the information the author provides in words. The complex graphs and maps that our students encounter are also extension images.

Brainstorming Activity: Emphasizing the Purpose of Different Images

We want our students to understand that images can serve a variety of purposes, so let's begin by asking our students to brainstorm as a class the importance of images in their science text. What purpose do the images serve for the reader? Do the images provide additional information for the reader, emphasize what is in the text, or just make the text more appealing? When students create science projects, write in their journals, or make PowerPoint presentations, do they ever choose to use any of these types of images, and if so, why? Are all types of images equally valuable? Why might an author include an organizational illustration versus just using a representational illustration when the text discusses the stages of digestion?

To begin the brainstorming activity, list the four purposes for images on a whiteboard or large sheet of paper. Provide each small group of students with sticky notes and ask them to locate one example of each type of image in a science text by placing the sticky note on the corresponding page. It may be that images representing all four purposes aren't in their text, but they can try to find as many types as possible. Afterward, have each group share the four images it found. Lots of conversation can occur with this activity. Was it easier to find some types of images than others? Were there any instances when students felt that a different type of image might have made more sense with the text? When students create texts or science projects, how can this information impact the images they use to convey information?

Types and Uses

In order to discuss anything with accuracy, we have to have the appropriate vocabulary terms. For example, can you imagine trying to create a project or invent something if *tool* were the only term you knew for a building utensil? In order to invent or create most projects, we have to know at the very least that the basic building tools include hammers, pliers, and screwdrivers. Nobody can use tools by merely asking for a *thingamajig*. The same is true for images. We can't compare and contrast the ways in which images convey information if we call them all *images*.

Categorizing the Types of Images

Just as we would never use the term *story* to refer to both narrative and informational text, we don't want to use the generic terms *picture* and *image* to refer to specific illustrations, photographs, graphs, charts, and diagrams. Steve Moline (2011) groups images into five categories. These categories are shown in Figure 5.4.

As Moline points out, some categories of images are less complex than others. The simplest of diagrams only labels parts of an image. These diagrams also include images where the diagram is created to scale and the image includes a ruler. This includes maps, which often require the viewer to think about the

CATEGORIES OF IMAGES*

Type	Brief Explanation	Examples
Simple diagrams (includes maps)	Drawings with labels; in maps, viewer typically looks down	Picture glossaries, scale diagrams, bird's-eye views, other maps
Analytic diagrams	Show items that are too small or hidden to be seen	Enlargements, cutaways, cross sections, exploded diagrams, block diagrams
Process diagrams	Show a sequence of events	Time lines, storyboards, flowcharts
Structure diagrams	Show relationships	Webs, trees, tables, Venn diagrams
Graphs	"About" numbers	Simple, bar/column, line, pie

*Based on categories in *I See What You Mean* (Moline 2011).

◀ FIGURE 5.4

view of the person looking at it, and often this is a view where the person is standing above the map and looking down on it. Analytic diagrams include cutaways, where a layer is removed. It isn't unusual in science to see an image of a frog without the top layer so our students can see the internal organs. This also includes exploded diagrams such as our students might see when assembling something with an enormous number of parts, and block diagrams, in which a square block is removed from the object to show what is inside.

These are all more concrete images our students might encounter in science texts or choose to create to share scientific information. The other categories of images show sequences, structures, and relationships between ideas or data.

> » Process or sequence diagrams include those that show a sequence of events, such as time lines, storyboards, and flowcharts. Many of our students have probably been creating these in science since they were in the younger grades, but it can be helpful to draw attention to the images and talk about the information they convey to the viewer.
> » Structure diagrams, such as Venn, web, and tree diagrams, show relationships. Chances are these images are not entirely unfamiliar to our students, but we should ensure that our students can accurately identify these types as they discuss the images in science texts.
> » Finally, there are graphs. Graphs are often seen in many content areas, and typically they include numbers. In science, our students will often encounter bar, line, and pie graphs in text.

Understanding Types of Images: Image Sort

Begin by dividing the class into small groups of students, and ask each group to bring in a variety of images that they find interesting in science texts, including websites, trade books, magazines, newspapers, and journals. For print texts, they may have to photocopy the images unless students can bring in the actual texts. Be sure to encourage students to find images that they feel look interesting, eye-catching, and even difficult to understand.

On a specified day, ask students to bring in all the samples they could find. Begin by having students brainstorm in their groups any similarities or differences among the images. See if students can group their examples by those characteristics and ask them to jot down a title for each category that states the similarity or commonality. For example, students might find that several images show the passage of time (process diagrams). Ask students to think about the type of information each image seeks to convey. Then have small groups share their ideas for categories. Did multiple groups of students create similar categories? What about the images may make them easier or more difficult to understand? Now, divide a large sheet of butcher paper into five sections. Label each section with one of the categories shown in Figure 5.4. Briefly introduce each category. Acknowledge that while there may be many ways to categorize the images they brought to class, these five categories are broad enough to include any images they may encounter. As a class, discuss in depth one category at a time, and see if each small group of students can share one example of each type of picture and then place it in the corresponding section. This wall chart can serve as a type of local text that reinforces the various types of images students find in science text.

When we use the correct terms to talk about images, the terms will become part of our students' listening vocabulary. Then as we ask questions about images, and students use the terms to answer questions in class and even talk with classmates, the terms will become part of their speaking vocabulary.

Strategies for Comprehending Images

We know that the images our students encounter often require that the reader not only examine the information in a visual representation but also draw inferences from it (Fang 2004; Lemke 1998). Just as students need strategies for comprehending the written word, they must be taught how to comprehend images and synthesize the information they gain from the images with that which they gain from words in the text they are reading. As we work with our students, we can review comprehension strategies they currently use with words and discuss which ones can also work with images. Let's think about how we read and gain information from the words in a science text and see how that relates to viewing images.

> » *Reading is rarely quick and easy.* Often we must read and reread words in a science text in order to gain meaning. Likewise, we must also use that same philosophy with reading images. We must take the time to view and review images. As we do this, we must think about the information in the text and how it relates to the image.

» *Comprehension requires monitoring.* If we read something, and it doesn't make sense, we stop. The goal of reading words is to make sense, or meaning. The same is true with images. When we look at images, the images must also make sense and fit in with what we are reading. If they don't make sense, then we must go back into the text and image and search for meaning. We can't just continue on with our reading.

» *We read science text to gain information.* Our purpose is to take away information when we read science text. Therefore, we need to focus on what we are reading. This differs from the narrative texts we read purely for fun, where we want to become part of the story experience. Therefore, we have to remember we are reading scientific images for information, which typically means few distractions and a focus on analyzing the information in the images.

» *We look at the bigger picture.* If we don't understand every word we read, we look at what we do know and see if we can determine what the unfamiliar words or phrases mean. Likewise, we can look at images and figure out what we do know. Then we can try to fill in the parts that are unfamiliar using information from the text.

» *We read critically.* We don't take words at face value, and likewise, we want to examine images we encounter to make sure that the author is not trying to sway us through information in the image. Are our eyes drawn to certain aspects of the image because of emotional words in the text or the use of color or font? Has an author altered the labels or axes on a graph to present a misleading result?

Along with interpreting images themselves, our students need to be able to synthesize the information in the image with the information they gain from words. For example, as a student reads through a science text and comes to an image, the student must first focus attention on the image and then be able to go back to the text and understand how the information from that image relates to the rest of the text.

Modeling Thought Processes

As teachers, we often use the think-aloud strategy with text because the strategy allows us to make our thought processes explicit to students as we read. We can also model a think-aloud so that our students understand how to approach images they encounter in science text.

Begin by selecting a chunk of science text that contains images. It may be a short trade book, a photocopy of an online article, or a chapter in their textbook. As you orally read the text to students, you will model how you think about and interpret the images. The following is an example of how a think-aloud with images would work.

Preview the chunk of science text and put sticky notes near images or references to images in the text that you want to emphasize. Write down your thoughts on those sticky notes. What strategies do you use when you get to those points in the text to help you comprehend? What steps do you take to interpret the images and what do you look for when you see the images? You can't teach everything at once to students. Focus on a few key points per image.

Your sticky notes may contain points such as these:

» What type of information do I expect to gain from this image?
» How does the information in this image tie to what I just read in the text? Does it decorate, reinforce, organize, or extend the text?
» Is there anything in this image that is confusing?
» What are a few key points that I can take away from this image?
» Is the image distorted to emphasize certain information?

The next step is to introduce the think-aloud to students. Explain to students that as you read the text, you are going to model the types of questions that go through your mind when you encounter images in scientific text and try to make sense of their role in the text. As you read the text, be sure to include relevant terms such as *arrows*, *sequential steps*, *headings*, *subheadings*, *text boxes*, *captions*, and *titles*. As you read, consider pointing, highlighting, using sticky notes, or annotating so that students follow your thought processes during the think-aloud.

Since we want students to learn to successfully view a wide variety of images, we need to strategically choose when to use a think-aloud. For example, we might use think-alouds if we question whether our students have a great deal of experience with a specific type of image, if the image is a type that we don't remember seeing in prior science text, or if we notice that our students are having trouble understanding a chunk of text containing an image.

We model our thought processes so that our students understand how to think about images. Then as our students internalize the process and questions to consider, we gradually withdraw our support, and the students learn to monitor their understanding of images. Instead of asking the questions, we can have students tell us what they would mark on the page and what questions come to their minds. As students become familiar with the think-aloud strategy, they can also model their thinking for classmates to see. A student who is able to understand a complex image, or understand an image that appears to be creating difficulties for classmates, can explain how to synthesize the words and image to understand the image.

Encouraging Critical Analysis

As our students begin analyzing images in science texts, we can scaffold them with questions and comments to ensure that they critically consume the information in the image. The following questions are examples of the types of questions we can ask our students:

» Why do you think the author(s) chose to represent the information in that manner? Why might an author choose to use one type of image instead of another (e.g., a cutaway diagram versus other types of diagrams)?

» Did the author(s) use images to extend the information in the text, organize the information we see in text, or reinforce important points in the written words?

» Is the type of image we see the most effective way to represent information, or is there a different type of image that would be more beneficial? If another type would be better, what would make it better?

» How important is the placement of an image in relation to the corresponding text? (Perhaps it is difficult to understand the information in the image because a reader has to keep looking back in the text to reread the information and then look ahead at the image.) Should the image be closer to the textual information?

» Compare several images that share information on the same scientific concept. For example, can we gain the same information from a picture of a plant growing and a diagram explaining through arrows the photosynthesis cycle?

For digital technologies, we might also consider the following additional questions:

» How does the creator of the text use music, graphics, animation, color, texture, and other aspects in the images?
» Do the special effects the author uses with the images strengthen scientific understanding or do the effects interfere and cause the viewer to lose focus on the content?
» Has there been manipulation of the image in some way? If so, why might the author have chosen to manipulate it?
» Is information distorted in the graph or diagram? If so, how might the distortion cause a misunderstanding? Why might the author have done that?

Before Moving on—Beyond This Book!

My goal with this book has been to strengthen our students' scientific knowledge and make scientific content accessible. While we want to actively involve our students in hands-on science experiments, we also want them to be aware of and understand discoveries that are happening all over the world. The best way we can do that is by exposing our students to diverse science texts, building their scientific vocabulary, showing them how to best approach scientific text, and focusing on the important role images play in the field of science.

There is no way to prepare our students for every scientific text they will encounter. Likewise, it's impossible to teach our students every scientific vocabulary term they must know or every scientific image they will encounter. However, we can arm our students with the tools they need to be independent learners. Our students need to be prepared not only for the science class as we know it today but for future science classes and the world beyond.

APPENDIX A   Suggested Twitter Chats

#CCSSchat: If you want to talk to others about the Common Core State Standards, then be sure to join this Twitter chat. Chats occur bimonthly on Sunday nights.

#edchat: This is one of the most popular educational chats. Chats occur on Tuesdays at 12:00 p.m. and 7:00 p.m. (EST).

#edtechchat: This chat will appeal to teachers who want to know more about using educational technology. Chats occur on Mondays at 8:00 p.m. (EST).

#flipclass: Maybe you've heard the term *flipped classroom* or are interested in implementing it in your school. In a flipped classroom, students complete the work traditionally done in class (i.e., lectures) outside of class, and activities which might typically be considered homework (i.e., exercises, projects) are done during class. If this idea is of interest to you, this may be the Twitter chat to attend. Chats occur on Mondays at 8:00 p.m. (EST).

#IRAChat: While the International Reading Association has chats about various topics related to literacy, some of them also apply specifically to science. Science authors such as Seymour Simon have cohosted chats. Chats occur the second Thursday of each month at 8:00 p.m. (EST).

#ls_chat: If you are looking to discuss life science, then join this life science Twitter chat that occurs biweekly on Wednesdays at 10:00 a.m. (PST).

#CitSciChat: This monthly chat joins citizen scientists, students, and others to share ideas and resources regarding citizen science. The chats are held the last Wednesday of every month from 7:00 to 8:00 p.m. (GMT).

#StuSciChat: This chat connects high school students and scientists. It's a great way to provide students with an opportunity to talk with those in the field of science and discuss ideas.

#ASEChat: The Association for Science Education chat is a weekly online chat that occurs on Mondays nights from 8:00 to 9:00 UK time. Given that UK time is five hours later than EST, it isn't realistic that U.S. teachers will be able to participate live in this Twitter chat. However, like most Twitter chats, teachers can view the highlights and many valuable resources at any time after the weekly chat ends.

#SciChat: This is a chat for science teachers at all levels and is held at 9:00 p.m. (EST) on Tuesdays. The chat covers all topics related to science and the teaching of science.

APPENDIX B   Science Trade Book Evaluation Guide

AREA OF FOCUS	NOTES

Science Content

❍ Were experts consulted?

❍ Does it include background info on author and/or illustrator?

❍ Is there any misleading information?

❍ Are the information and copyright current?

❍ Is it free of stereotypes?

Images

❍ Are the illustrations realistic?

❍ Do the photographs support the text, and are they accompanied by credits?

❍ Are the drawings accurate in scale?

Writing

❍ Is it engaging for students?

❍ Is there a logical presentation?

❍ Does the text include precise scientific terminology?

Informational Text Features

❍ Does it contain useful labels, captions, sidebars, and/or charts and keys?

❍ Is there a useful table of contents and/ or glossary?

❍ Does it use different typefaces for emphasis?

Overall Design

❍ Are the layout and format appropriate?

❍ Is it appealing to students?

APPENDIX C Digital Science Text Evaluation Guide

AREA OF FOCUS	NOTES

Science Content

- ❍ Is there any background information about the author?
- ❍ Is there any misleading information?
- ❍ Are the information and copyright current?
- ❍ Is it free of stereotypes?
- ❍ Does the information extend beyond the text?

Images

- ❍ Are the illustrations realistic?
- ❍ Do the photographs support the text, and are they accompanied by credits?
- ❍ Are the drawings accurate in scale?
- ❍ Are there interactive visuals?

Writing

- ❍ Is it engaging for students?
- ❍ Is there a logical presentation?
- ❍ Does it include precise scientific terminology?
- ❍ Are the grammar and spelling correct?

Overall Design

- ❍ Are the layout and format appropriate?
- ❍ Is it appealing to students?

Text Access

- ❍ Is it easy to use?
- ❍ Does it work with various browsers?

APPENDIX D   Key Science Terms Chart

Multi-meaning	Tier Two	Tier Three

APPENDIX E   Group Knowledge Rating Sheet

Science Term	1 pt.	3 pts.	5 pts.	Points
	Unfamiliar	Know a Little What do you know?	Know It Well / Can Teach It Write the definition.	

Science Term	1 pt.	3 pts.	5 pts.	Points
	Unfamiliar	Know a Little What do you know?	Know It Well / Can Teach It Write the definition.	

Science Term	1 pt.	3 pts.	5 pts.	Points
	Unfamiliar	Know a Little What do you know?	Know It Well / Can Teach It Write the definition.	

Group Knowledge Rating Sheet page 2

Science Term	1 pt.	3 pts.	5 pts.	Points
	Unfamiliar	Know a Little What do you know?	Know It Well / Can Teach It Write the definition.	

Science Term	1 pt.	3 pts.	5 pts.	Points
	Unfamiliar	Know a Little What do you know?	Know It Well / Can Teach It Write the definition.	

Individual student points _____
Group points _____
Class points _____

APPENDIX F   Keyword Template

Science Term:_____ Keyword:_____

Definition of science term: _____

_____

_____

Visual:

APPENDIX G   Informational Text Features Chart

Science Topic:_____

Features	Book 1	Book 2	Book 3	Book 4
Appendix				
Captions				
Electronic Menus				
Flowcharts				
Fonts				
Glossary				
Graphs/Charts				
Headings/Subheadings				
Hyperlinks				
Icons				
Index				
Labeled Diagrams				
Maps and Keys				
Sidebars				
Table of Contents				
Tables				
Time Lines				

Book 1:_____

Book 2:_____

Book 3:_____

Book 4:_____

APPENDIX H Looking Through the Lens

Scientists love to take a closer look at things by viewing them through a microscope's lens. Let's take a closer look at scientific texts by also Looking Through the Lens at them. Write down the titles of three texts on a topic at the bottom of the page. Then think about *each* of the questions under the Areas to Analyze. Jot your notes in the correct column. What did you learn about the texts?

Areas to Analyze	Text 1	Text 2	Text 3
Reason: Why was this science text written? Did the author want to entertain/persuade/inform?			
Type of Science Text: Is this a digital text or a printed text? Is this a brochure, article, press release, or some other type of text?			
Important Details: Are important details included? What text features were used? Are there emotional words used to persuade or show bias?			
Source: Who wrote, illustrated, and published the piece? Do we know anything about the source?			
Time of Text Creation: Is this piece current? If not, is there reason to question the accuracy of the information?			

Text 1: _____

Text 2: _____

Text 3: _____

Bibliography

Ajayi, L. 2009. "English as a Second Language Learners' Exploration of Multimodal Texts in a Junior High School." *Journal of Adolescent and Adult Literacy* 52 (7): 585–95.

Altieri, Jennifer L. 2011. *Content Counts! Developing Disciplinary Literacy Skills, K–6*. Newark, DE: International Reading Association.

———. 2014. *Powerful Content Connections: Nurturing Readers, Writers, and Thinkers in Grades K–3*. Newark, DE: International Reading Association.

Anders, Patricia L., and Candace S. Boss. 1986. "Semantic Feature Analysis: An Interaction Strategy for Vocabulary Development and Text Comprehension." *Journal of Reading* 29 (7): 610–16.

Armstrong, Joseph E., and Glenn E. Collier. 1990. *Science in Biology: An Introduction*. Prospect Heights, IL: Waveland.

Atkinson, Richard C. 1975. "Mnemotechnics in Second-Language Learning." *American Psychologist* 30 (8): 821–28.

Atkinson, Richard C., and Michael R. Raugh. 1975. "An Application of the Mnemonic Keyword Method to Acquisition of a Russian Vocabulary." *Journal of Experimental Psychology* 1 (2): 126–33.

Atkinson, Terry S., Melissa N. Matusevich, and Lisa Huber. 2009. "Making Science Trade Book Choices for Elementary Classrooms." *The Reading Teacher* 62 (6): 484–97.

Avery, Carol. 2003. "Nonfiction Books: Naturals for the Primary Level." In *Making Facts Come Alive: Choosing and Using Nonfiction Literature, K–8*, 2nd ed., edited by Rosemary A. Bamford and Janice V. Kristo, 235–46. Norwood, MA: Christopher-Gordon.

Bamford, Rosemary A., Janice V. Kristo, and Anna Lyon. 2002. "Facing Facts: Nonfiction in the Primary Classroom." *The New England Reading Association Journal* 38 (2): 8–15.

Bean, Thomas W., and Ashley L. Bishop. 1992. "Polar Opposites: A Strategy for Guiding Students' Critical Reading and Discussion." In *Reading in the Content Areas: Improving Classroom Instruction*, 3rd ed., edited by Ernest K. Dishner, John E. Readence, and David W. Moore, 247–254. Dubuque, IA: Kendall/Hunt.

Beck, Isabel L., and Margaret G. McKeown. 1985. "Teaching Vocabulary: Making the Instruction Fit the Goal." *Educational Perspectives* 23 (1): 11–15.

———. 1988. "Toward Meaningful Accounts in History Texts for Young Learners." *Educational Researcher* 17 (6): 31–39.

Blachowicz, Camille L. Z. 1986. "Making Connections: Alternatives to the Vocabulary Notebook." *Journal of Reading* 29 (7): 643–49.

Blachowicz, Camille L. Z., Peter J. L. Fisher, Donna Ogle, and Susan Watts-Taffe. 2006. "Vocabulary: Questions from the Classroom." *Reading Research Quarterly* 41 (4): 524–39.

Bos, Candace S., Patricia L. Anders, Dorothy Filip, and Lynne E. Jaffe. 2001. "The Effects of an Interactive Instructional Strategy for Enhancing Reading Comprehension and Content Area Learning for Students with Learning Disabilities." *Journal of Learning Disabilities* 22 (6): 384–90.

Broemmel, Amy D., and Kristin T. Rearden. 2006. "Should Teachers Use the Teachers' Choices Books in Science Classes?" *The Reading Teacher* 60 (3): 254–65.

Carney, Russell N., and Joel R. Levin. 2002. "Pictorial Illustrations *Still* Improve Students' Learning from Text." *Educational Psychology Review* 14 (1): 5–26.

Coleman, Julianne M., Erin M. McTigue, and Laura B. Smolkin. 2011. "Elementary Teachers' Use of Graphical Representations in Science Teaching." *Journal of Science Teacher Education* 22 (7): 613–43.

Conderman, Greg, and C. Sheldon Woods. 2008. "Science Instruction: An Endangered Species." *Kappa Delta Pi Record* 44 (2): 76–80.

Decker, Todd, Gerald Summers, and Lloyd Barrow. 2007. "The Treatment of Geological Time and the History of Life on Earth in High School Biology Textbooks." *The American Biology Teacher* 69 (7): 401–5.

Donovan, Carol A., and Laura B. Smolkin. 2001. "Genre and Other Factors Influencing Teachers' Book Selections for Science Instruction." *Reading Research Quarterly* 36 (4): 412–40.

Duke, Nell K. 2000. "3.6 Minutes per Day: The Scarcity of Informational Texts in First Grade." *Reading Research Quarterly* 35 (2): 202–24.

Eilam, Billie, and Yael Poyas. 2008. "Learning with Multiple Representations: Extending Multimedia Learning Beyond the Lab." *Learning and Instruction* 18 (4): 368–78.

Fang, Zhihui. 2004. "Scientific Inquiry: A Functional Linguistic Perspective." *Science Education* 89 (2): 335–47.

Fisher, Douglas, and Nancy Frey. 2012. "Close Reading in Elementary Schools." *The Reading Teacher* 66 (3): 179–88.

Flood, James, and Diane Lapp. 1998. "Broadening Conceptualizations of Literacy: The Visual and Communicative Arts." *The Reading Teacher* 51 (4): 342–344.

Gill, Sharon Ruth. 2009. "What Teachers Need to Know About the 'New' Nonfiction." *The Reading Teacher* 63 (4): 260–67.

Good, Jessica J., Julie A. Woodzicka, and Lylan C. Wingfield. 2010. "The Effects of Gender Stereotypic and Counter-Stereotypic Textbook Images on Science Performance." *The Journal of Social Psychology* 150 (2): 132–47.

Graves, Michael F., and Susan M. Watts-Taffe. 2002. "The Place of Word Consciousness in a Research-Based Vocabulary Program." In *What Research Has to Say About Reading Instruction*, edited by Alan E. Farstrup and S. Jay Samuels, 140–65. Newark, DE: International Reading Association.

Haggard, Martha R. 1986. "The Vocabulary Self-Collection Strategy: Using Student Interest and World Knowledge to Enhance Vocabulary Growth." *Journal of Reading* 29 (7): 634–42.

Henke, Robin R., Xianglei Chen, and Gideon Goldman. 1999. "What Happens in Classrooms? Instructional Practices in Elementary and Secondary Schools, 1994–95." NCES 1999–348. Washington, DC: National Center for Education Statistics, US Department of Education. Retrieved May 25, 2014, from http://nces.ed.gov/pubs99/1999348.pdf.

Hubber, Peter, Russell Tytler, and Filocha Haslam. 2010. "Teaching and Learning About Force with a Representational Focus: Pedagogy and Teacher Change." *Research in Science Education* 40 (1): 5–28.

Lee, Victor Raymond. 2008. "Getting the Picture: A Mixed-Methods Inquiry into How Visual Representations Are Interpreted by Students, Incorporated Within Textbooks, and Integrated into Middle School Science Classrooms." PhD diss., Northwestern University.

Lemke, Jay. 1998. "Multiplying Meaning: Visual and Verbal Semiotics in Scientific Text." In *Reading Science: Critical and Functional Perspectives on Discourses of Science*, edited by James R. Martin and Robert Veel, 87–113. London: Routledge.

Levin, Joel R. 1981. "On Functions of Pictures in Prose." In *Neuropsychological and Cognitive Processes in Reading*, edited by Francis J. Pirozzolo and Merlin C. Wittrock, 203–28. New York: Academic Press.

Luke, Carmen, Suzanne DeCastell, and Allan Luke. 1983. "Beyond Criticism: The Authority of the School Text." *Curriculum Inquiry* 13 (2): 111–27.

Maloch, Beth, James V. Hoffman, and Elizabeth U. Patterson. 2004. "Local Texts: Reading and Writing 'of the Classroom.'" In *The Texts in Elementary Classrooms*, edited by James V. Hoffman and Diane L. Schallert, 29–138. Mahwah, NJ: Erlbaum.

Manderino, Michael. 2007. "Integrating the Visual: Student Strategies for Multiple Text Synthesis." Paper presented at the National Reading Conference, November 28–December 1, Austin, TX.

Martins, Isabel. 2002. "Visual Imagery in School Science Texts." In *The Psychology of Science Text Comprehension*, edited by Jose Otero, Jose A. León, and Arthur C. Graesser, 73–90. Mahwah, NJ: Lawrence Erlbaum.

Marzano, Robert J., and Debra J. Pickering. 2005. *Building Academic Vocabulary: Teacher's Manual.* Alexandria, VA: Association for Supervision and Curriculum Development.

Mattox, Steve. 2008. "How Gender and Race of Geologists Are Portrayed in Physical Geology Textbooks." *Journal of Geoscience Education* 56 (2): 156–59.

McKeown, Margaret G., Isabel L. Beck, and Mary Jo Worthy. 1993. "Grappling with Text Ideas: Questioning the Author." *The Reading Teacher* 46 (7): 560–66.

Moline, Steve. 2011. *I See What You Mean: Visual Literacy, K–8.* Portland, ME: Stenhouse.

Morrison, Judith A., and Terrell A. Young. 2008. "Using Science Trade Books to Support Inquiry in the Elementary Classroom." *Childhood Education* 84 (4): 204–8.

National Governors Association Center for Best Practices and Council of Chief State School Officers. 2010. *Common Core State Standards for English Language Arts and Literacy in History/Social Studies, Science, and Technical Subjects.* Washington, DC: Authors.

NGSS Lead States. 2013. *Next Generation Science Standards: For States, by States.* Washington, DC: National Academies Press.

National Science Resources Center. 2006a. "Bicycles Roll In." In *Motion and Design* (part of the Science and Technology Concepts™ program), 32–33. Burlington, NC: Carolina Biological Supply Company.

——— . 2006b. "The Mechanics of Bikes." In *Motion and Design* (part of the Science and Technology Concepts™ program), 34–36. Burlington, NC: Carolina Biological Supply Company.

Ogan-Bekiroglu, Feral. 2007. "To What Degree Do the Currently Used Physics Textbooks Meet the Expectations?" *Journal of Science Teacher Education* 18 (4): 599–628.

Ogle, Donna M. 1986. "K-W-L: A Teaching Model That Develops Active Reading of Expository Text." *The Reading Teacher* 39 (6): 564–70.

Padak, Nancy, Evangeline Newton, Timothy Rasinski, and Rick M. Newton. 2008. "Getting to the Root of Word Study: Teaching Latin and Greek Word Roots in Elementary and Middle Grades." In *What Research Has to Say About Vocabulary Instruction*, edited by Alan E. Farstrup and S. Jay Samuels, 6–31. Newark, DE: International Reading Association.

Pentimonti, Jill M., Tricia A. Zucker, Laura M. Justice, and Joan N. Kaderavek. 2010. "Informational Text Use in Preschool Classroom Read-Alouds." *The Reading Teacher* 63 (8): 656–65.

Pérez-Echeverría, Maria-Puy, Yolanda Postigo, and Ana Pecharroman. 2009. "Graphicacy: University Students' Skills in Translating Information." In *Representational Systems and Practices as Learning Tools*, edited by Christopher Andersen, Nora Scheuer, Maria-Puy Pérez-Echeverría, and Eva V. Teubal, 209–24. Boston: Sense.

Phillip, Abby. "What Is Enterovirus 68, the Mysterious Illness that Is Sickening Hundreds of Children?" *The Washington Post.* Sept. 8, 2014.

Pringle, Rose M., and Linda Leonard Lamme. 2005. "Using Picture Storybooks to Support Young Children's Science Learning." *Reading Horizons* 46 (1): 1–15.

Rice, Diana C. 2002. "Using Trade Books in Teaching Elementary Science: Facts and Fallacies." *The Reading Teacher* 55 (6): 552–65.

Robinson, Francis Pleasant. 1946. *Effective Study.* New York: Harper and Row.

Rosenblatt, Louise M. 1938. *Literature as Exploration.* New York: Appleton-Century Crofts.

Santa, Carol Minnick. 1988. *Content Reading Including Study Systems: Reading, Writing and Studying Across the Curriculum.* Dubuque, IA: Kendall/Hunt.

Shanahan, Timothy, and Cynthia Shanahan. 2008. "Teaching Disciplinary Literacy to Adolescents: Rethinking Content-Area Literacy." *Harvard Educational Review* 78 (1): 40–59.

Slough, Scott W., Erin M. McTigue, Suyeon Kim, and Susan K. Jennings. 2010. "Science Textbooks' 2010 Use of Graphical Representation: A Descriptive Analysis of Four Sixth Grade Science Texts." *Reading Psychology* 31 (3): 301–25.

Songer, Nancy B., and Marcia C. Linn. 1991. "How Do Students' Views of Science Influence Knowledge Integration?" *Journal of Research in Science Teaching* 28 (9): 761–84.

Taba, Hilda. 1967. *Teacher's Handbook for Elementary Social Studies.* Reading, MA: Addison-Wesley.

Thompson, Clive. 2011. "Why Johnny Can't Search." *Wired*, November 1. Available at www.wired.com/2011/11/st_thompson_searchresults/.

Treagust, David F. 2007. "General Instructional Methods and Strategies." In *Handbook of Research on Science Education*, edited by Sandra K. Abell and Norman G. Lederman, 373–91. Mahwah, NJ: Lawrence Erlbaum.

Vacca, Richard T., and Jo Anne L. Vacca. 2002. *Content Area Reading: Literacy and Learning Across the Curriculum.* Boston: Allyn and Bacon.

———. 2005. *Content Area Reading: Literacy and Learning Across the Curriculum.* 8th ed. Boston: Pearson Education.

Van Meter, Peggy, Maja Aleksic, Ana Schwartz, and Joanna Garner. 2006. "Learner-Generated Drawing as a Strategy for Learning from Content Area Text." *Contemporary Educational Psychology* 31 (2): 142–66.

Vaughn, Sally, Sharon Crawley, and Lee Mountain. 1979. "A Multiple-Modality Approach to Word Study: Vocabulary Scavenger Hunts." *The Reading Teacher* 32 (4): 434–37.

Weiss, Iris R., and Joan D. Pasley. 2004. "What Is High Quality Instruction?" *Improving Achievement in Math and Science* 61 (5): 24–28.

Wiley, David, and Elissa Barr. 2007. "Health Education Textbook Adoption in Texas: A Lesson in Politics and Morality." *American Journal of Health Education* 38 (5): 295–300.

Winters Keegan, Rebecca. 2006. "Looking for a Lab-Coat Idol." *Time* 167 (7): 26–27.

Yopp, Hallie Kay, and Ruth Helen Yopp. 2003. "Ten Important Words: Identifying the Big Ideas in Informational Text." *Journal of Content Area Reading* 2 (1): 7–13.

Yore, Larry D. 2004. "Why Do Future Scientists Need to Study the Language Arts?" In *Crossing Borders in Literacy and Science Instruction: Perspectives on Theory and Practice*, edited by E. Wendy Saul, 71–94. Newark, DE: International Reading Association.

Zygouris-Coe, Vicky, Matthew B. Wiggins, and Lourdes H. Smith. 2004. "Engaging Students with Text: The 3-2-1 Strategy." *The Reading Teacher* 58 (4): 381–84.

Zywica, Jolene, and Kimberley Gomez. 2008. "Annotating to Support Learning in the Content Areas: Teaching and Learning Science." *Journal of Adolescent and Adult Literacy* 52 (2): 155–65.

Websites Cited

http://blogs.smithsonianmag.com/science/2010/12/great-science-books-for-the-little-ones/

http://infogr.am

www.dawcl.com

www.donorschoose.org

www.easel.ly

www.nces.ed.gov/nceskids/graphing/classic/

www.nces.ed.gov/nceskids/graphing/classic/

www.nsta.org/publications/ostb/
www.popularscience.co.uk/?cat=106
www.reading.org/Resources/Booklists/TeachersChoices.aspx
www.reading.org/Resources/Booklists/YoungAdultsChoices.aspx
www.tagxedo.com
www.thesaurus.com
www.tingoed.com
www.wordcentral.com
www.wordle.net

Children's Books Cited

Applegate, Katherine. 2012. *The One and Only Ivan*. New York: HarperCollins.

Blechman, Nicholas. 2014. *Information Graphics: Animal Kingdom*. Somerville, MA: Candlewick.

Buzzeo, Toni. 2013. *But I Read It on the Internet*. Madison, WI: Upstart Books.

Cole, Joanna. 1990. *The Magic School Bus Inside the Human Body*. New York: Scholastic.

Komiya, Teruyuki. 2009. *Life-Size Zoo*. New York: Seven Footer.

Korman, Gordon. 2011. *Unsinkable*. Titanic: Book One. New York: Scholastic.

Pringle, Laurence. 2010. *Cicadas! Strange and Wonderful*. Honesdale, PA: Boyds Mills.

Scieszka, Jon. 1995. *Math Curse*. New York: Viking Juvenile.

———. 2004. *Science Verse*. New York: Viking Juvenile.

Shields, Carol Diggory, and Richard Thompson. 2003. *Brainjuice: Science, Fresh Squeezed!* San Francisco: Chronicle Books.

Simon, Seymour. 2008. *Gorillas*. New York: HarperCollins.